a brief history of gardening

a brief history of gardening

neil fairbairn

RODALE

WE INSPIRE AND ENABLE PEOPLE TO IMPROVE THEIR LIVES AND THE WORLD AROUND THEM

Editor: Jennifer Hornsby

Cover and Book Designer: Marcella Bove-Huttie

Contributing Designer: Patricia Field

Illustrator: Edwin Fotheringham

Photography Editor: Lyn Horst

Photography Assistant: Jackie Ney

Layout Designers: Daniel MacBride, Donna Rossi

Copy Editors: Erana Bumbardatore, Linda Brunner

Manufacturing Coordinator: Patrick T. Smith

Color Output Specialist: Dale Mack

Indexer: Lina Burton

Editorial Assistance: Kerrie A. Cadden

Design Assistance: Susan A. Davis

RODALE ORGANIC LIVING BOOKS

Executive Editor: Kathleen DeVanna Fish

Executive Creative Director: Christin Gangi

Art Director: Patricia Field

Content Assembly Manager: Robert V. Anderson Jr.

Studio Manager: Leslie M. Keefe

Copy Manager: Nancy N. Bailey

Director, Production Control/Rodale Products: Paul Snyder

We're always happy to hear from you. For questions or comments concerning the editorial content of this book, please write to:

Rodale Book Readers' Service

33 East Minor Street

Emmaus, PA 18098

Look for other Rodale books wherever books are sold. Or call us at (800) 848-4735.

For more information about Rodale Organic Gardening magazine and books, visit us at:

www.organicgardening.com

On the front of the jacket: *Rosa gallica aurelianensis* 'La Duchesse D'Orleans' from *Les Roses* by Pierre-Joseph Redouté (1759–1804). Provided by Newberry Library, Chicago/SuperStock.

On the back of the jacket: *Versailles: The Grove* by Jean-Baptiste Martin (1659-1735). Provided by A.K.G., Berlin/SuperStock

Library of Congress Cataloging-in-Publication Data

Fairbairn, Neil.

  A brief history of gardening / Neil Fairbairn.

    p. cm.

  Includes bibliographical references (p.   ) and index.

  ISBN 0–87596–863–5 (hardcover)

  1. Gardening—History. I. Title.

SB451 .F14 2001

635'.09—dc21   00–011855

Distributed in the book trade by St. Martin's Press

2 4 6 8 10 9 7 5 3 1   hardcover

To my father,
Harold Williams Fairbairn,
who taught me nothing
about gardening but who
did grow the best tomatoes
I've ever eaten.

Contents

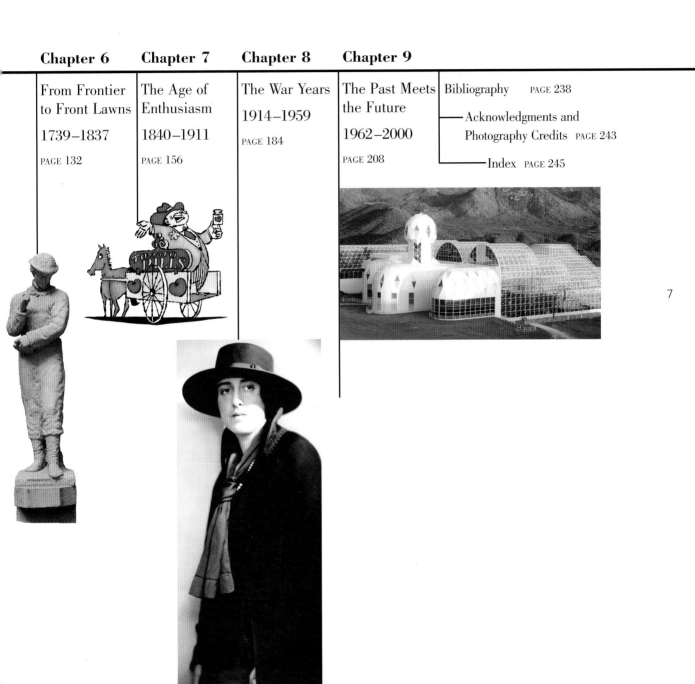

7

Introduction

Gardening is both the most natural and most unnatural of human activities. In what other way can humans respond so creatively to the rhythms of nature? Where but in the garden do

we feel such a kinship with the air, the soil, the sun, the rain, and the plants we nurture? But flip the coin to discover the backyard tyrant, for we gardeners destroy as passionately as we create. Gardeners chop, dig, and slash. We declare war on our enemies, and we decimate them.

Both of these characters—the disciple and the despot—have worked side by side throughout the history of gardening. At one extreme are those who treat the resources of the earth as their own private commodity, bringing destruction in their wake: the absentee landlords of the Roman Empire or the lords of agribusiness today. But near at hand are always the philosophers, the holy men and women, the practical farmers, and the visionary scientists, for whom stewardship of the living world is a sacred trust.

History offers no convenient stopping points; this book ends at the beginning of a new millennium, when the ambivalence of humanity toward the natural world is at a point of crisis. The only thing we can be certain of is that people will continue to garden. For our health, for our spirits, and for the world our children will inherit, we must cultivate our gardens with intelligence, care, and hope.

chapter one

Sowing the First Seeds

Just why men and women began to plant and nurture their own crops is one of the great mysteries of civilization. Did humans need to become farmers? According to some historians, the pressure of an increasing population or the shortage of available resources might have made the hunting-gathering life too difficult to maintain. Or perhaps—as others argue—it was just the opposite. Maybe agriculture started out as gardening—a pastime of people who were physically comfortable and had spare hours for all the planting, watering, and weeding involved.

However it came about, the gardening bug bit humanity all around the world, and at nearly the same time. In the Middle East, farmers coaxed wheat, barley, and beans out of the dry soil of the Fertile Crescent. In China, millet, rice, and soybeans added to the global diet. Farmers in the New World bred maize, potatoes, chiles, and—of course—cacao. All of these cultures were learning the same lessons independently, and within two or three thousand years of each other. In the broad span of Earth's history, that's just the blink of an eye.

While theories about agriculture's origins will come and go, there's no mystery about why people *continue* to garden. Ask anyone who has ever pored over a seed catalog or watered a newly sown bed. Gardeners are creating life; they are conserving life; above all, they are dreaming of life. Do we long for an irretrievable Eden, or maybe envision a garden paradise in a world to come? Gardening is more than a means of supplying sustenance or beauty; it is a form of communion with life itself.

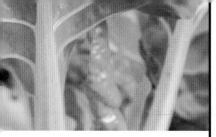

2.8 billion years ago

Photosynthesizing plants grow, causing free oxygen to occur in the atmosphere.

65 million years ago

The Cenozoic era begins. Dinosaurs become extinct. Birds, horses, and monkeys evolve.

24 million years ago

The first earthworms get busy turning decaying plant and animal matter into humus.

40,000 years ago

Hunter-gatherers harvest grains and tubers with stone sickles and digging sticks.

430 million years ago

Plants take root on land.

4.6 billion years ago

Earth forms from a swirling mass of gases and dust.

250 million years ago

The Mezozoic era, the age of dinosaurs, begins. It will last 185 million years.

1.8 million years ago

The Quaternary period begins: Glaciers begin to advance and retreat, shaping the continents, forming lakes, and leaving soil deposits. *Homo erectus* will fashion stone tools.

500 million years ago

Fish swim in Earth's waters.

9000 B.C.

In the Fertile Crescent, farmers cultivate wheat.

12,000 B.C.

Humans discover how to light fires.

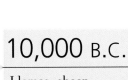

5000 B.C.

Maize is domesticated in Mexico.

6000 B.C.

Chinese farmers harvest millet.

7000 B.C.

Egyptian growers produce 500 medicinal plants.

10,000 B.C.

Llamas, sheep, goats, and pigs are domesticated around the globe.

4000 B.C.

Potatoes, lima beans, and squash grow in fields in the Andes.

6500 B.C.

Africans grow imported grains and legumes, and native sorghum and pearl millet.

5500 B.C.

Canal irrigation of Nile and Euphrates Rivers necessitates the growth of centralized governments.

4000 B.C.

Indus Valley farmers provide a balanced diet, raising wheat, barley, peas, sesame seeds, mangoes, dates, bananas, citrus, and grapes.

3000 B.C.

Oxen pull plows in Mesopotamia and Egypt, easing farmers' workloads.

Overgrazing and overworking the soil slowly turn North Africa's fertile grasslands and woodlands into the Sahara.

2640 B.C.

In China, Si Ling Chi turns silk into cloth.

2500 B.C.

Most Europeans plow their fields.

3500 B.C.

In the Middle East, time-conscious inventors create the sundial and the potter's wheel.

3500 B.C.

Northern Europeans learn to farm.

2700 B.C.

Early environmentalist Shen Nung mourns the deforestation of hills and erosion of the yellowing Yellow River.

1570 B.C.

Egyptians wall their gardens and develop the well-sweep.

1483 B.C.

Egyptian queen Hatshepsut hears voices of the gods and plants incense trees.

1000 B.C.

Incan farmers dig channels to irrigate fields and moderate the climate atop Andean peaks.

800 B.C.

The Book of Songs depicts Chinese agriculture and composting.

c.900 B.C.

The Etruscans come to Italy, by boat, from Asia Minor.

1350 B.C.

The Phoenicians use a 22-letter alphabet.

1500 B.C.

Allow farmland a sabbath year, preaches Moses.

1150 B.C.

Ramses III plants orchards and counts bouquet after bouquet after bouquet....

c.932 B.C.

Solomon builds the temple in Jerusalem.

2000 B.C.

Chinese farmers grow soybeans, Indians grow tea, and Arabians grow figs.

In the Beginning

40,000 B.C.

Early hunter-gatherers harvested roots and tubers with pointed digging sticks, which were sometimes weighted to break the hard earth more easily. Tools such as these would later evolve into primitive hoes for planting or weeding crops. With sickles made of flint, obsidian, or even clay, men and women harvested wild grains, holding the stalks carefully just below the tops to prevent seeds from shaking loose and spilling to the ground. The eventual use of metal would free farmers from their Stone Age tool kits, but for many years farming techniques would remain the same.

10,000 B.C.

Animal Companions

Sheep and goats were the earliest domestic animals, foraging alongside the gatherers of the Middle East as early as 10,000 B.C. The huge aurochs—fierce, wild oxen—would join the farmyard some centuries later, bred to become relatively peaceful cows. Pigs were kept by the first farmers who dug the soils of Europe, llamas carried loads for the people of Peru, and water buffalo labored for growers in the Indus Valley. These and other domestic animals served as useful supplements to the human diet, performed the heavy work, and reduced the pressure to hunt.

No one knows when a farmer first discovered that peas thrived where sheep had been penned or that edible greens sprang up where pigs had dug and fertilized the soil. For early farmers, manure was plentiful and all sources were acceptable. Seabird droppings, known as guano, have enriched the maize and beans of Peru and Ecuador since prehistoric times. Twenty-first-century gardeners still buy guano to use as an organic fertilizer in their backyard gardens.

The First Wheat Farmers

Men and women gathered wheat long before they grew it. In the lands of the Fertile Crescent, the wild einkorn and emmer wheats grew in abundance. Hunter-gatherers quickly learned that wheat could sustain life, tempting them to establish permanent settlements at a time when populations of the largest game animals were diminishing. Growing wheat was a nutritious move; wheat is rich in carbohydrates, proteins, and B vitamins.

Settling in sparsely forested valleys and hillsides where the wild wheat grew, early villagers harvested the grains with stone sickles and woven baskets. It must have been a frustrating task because the ears would often "shatter," sending kernels flying irretrievably to the earth. What people needed was wheat that stuck to the ear during harvesting.

Maybe the encounter was purely accidental, or perhaps an early horticulturist made and applied a few astute observations—whatever the reason, villagers in some of these scattered communities discovered a

Ancient African Agriculture

Archaeologists haven't unraveled the mystery of when farmers first began to cultivate plants in Africa. The first traces of an agricultural society are found on the banks of the Nile, in remains dating from 6500 B.C. These early farmers grew crops from the Middle East, including emmer wheat, barley, chickpeas, and lentils. But Africa had its own great indigenous crops, particularly sorghum and pearl millet, grains that thrived in the dry savanna south of the Sahara. Some early Africans may have had little incentive to plant and tend crops, though, because wild grains grew so densely that people could harvest them simply by swinging a wicker basket while walking through a field. One Western scientist estimated that even in the mid-twentieth century a family could gather 2,200 pounds (1,000 kilograms) of wild grains each year—hardly an incentive to plow the land.

strain of shatter-resistant wheat, and they encouraged its growth. These first farmers began actively cultivating their crops, saving some of their grain to use as seed, and then scattering it on land where they had seen wheat thrive in previous years. Grains dating back to 9000 B.C., which would be discovered later in certain villages, show clear signs of domestication: These grains grew on tough stalks and were plumper than their wild cousins, an indication that for numerous seasons farmers had been selecting the best seed based on the food it could provide for them.

Wheat was the most important of a number of crops cultivated by the early inhabitants of the Fertile Crescent. Domesticated barley was also sown in many of the first planted fields. And at about the same time as the earliest grain plantings, farmers began to sow and harvest lentils, chickpeas, and peas. These legumes were rich in lysine, a protein that wheat lacked. The result of having a variety of crops was a balanced diet that would fuel the great civilizations of the Middle East.

Early Chinese Staples

When more evidence is uncovered and examined, the Chinese will doubtless prove to have been among the earliest farmers in the world. In China's dry northwest, where the Yellow River cuts through soft, sandy soil, millet was the early staple. Eventually it was no rival to rice, which attracted the attention of farmers along China's great southern waterway, the Yangtze, at about the same time. Soybeans seem to have come under cultivation much later, probably after 2000 B.C. Analysis of ancient human skeletons shows that people who ate protein-rich soybeans were much healthier than their soy-free predecessors. Chinese farmers also seem to have understood—long before nitrogen-fixing bacteria had come under a microscope—that planting soybeans enriched the soil.

Investing in Irrigation

Knowing that plants need water is one thing. Getting it to them is quite another. Many early farming communities discovered that crops were a fickle investment if they didn't have a means of irrigation. In Mesopotamia and Egypt, the solution was relatively straightforward. By 5500 B.C., farmers had learned to water their crops year-round by cutting channels from the streams or rivers on which they had settled to the fields where they had planted their crops.

Irrigation came at a cost, however. The management of anything but the simplest system of canals required cooperation and centralized authority. With irrigation, the primitive farmer lost his political innocence, as complex, bureaucratic states developed on the banks of the Euphrates and the Nile. The politically dependent, interrelated world of agriculture and the more personal, private sphere of gardening had begun to part ways.

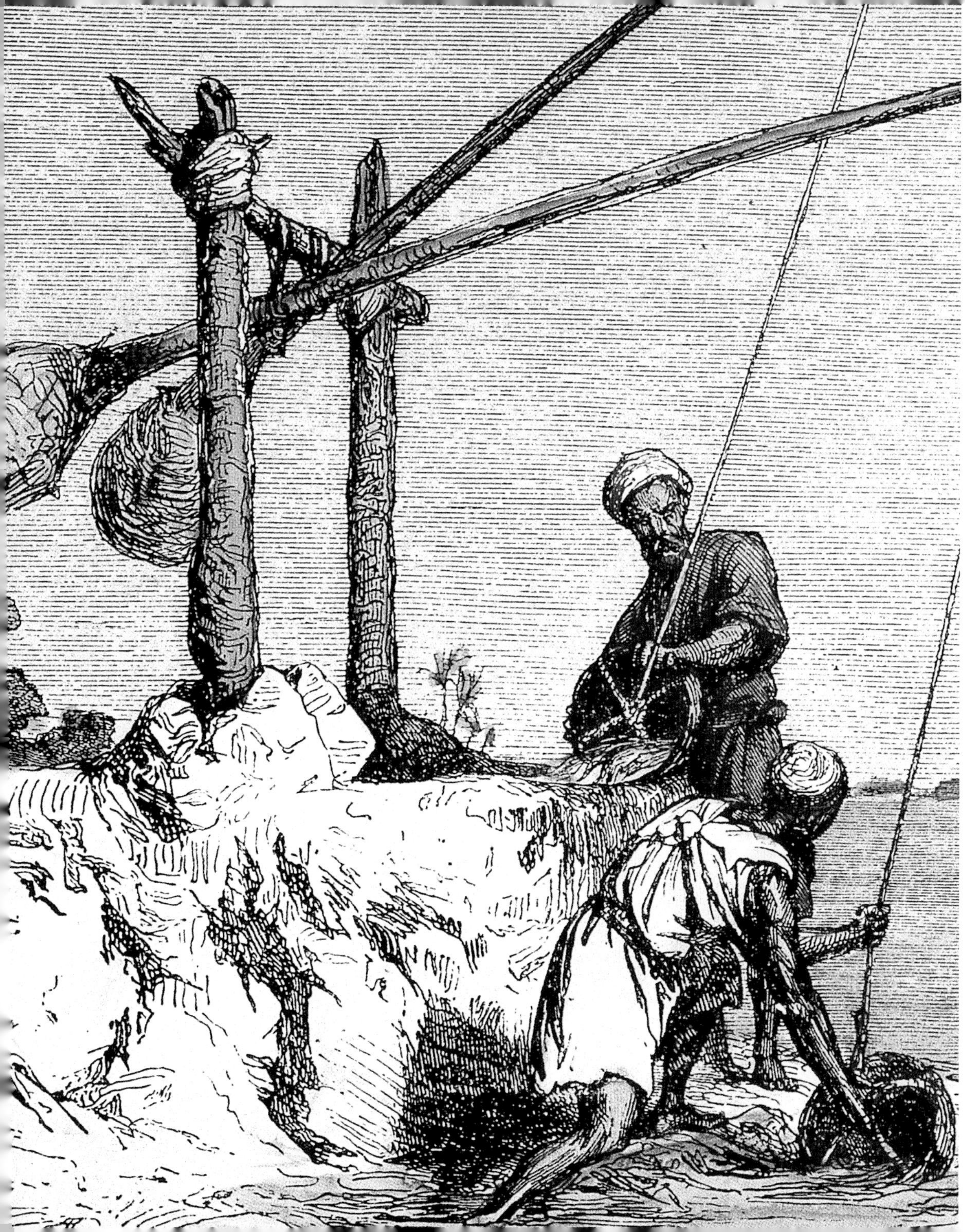

sowing
the
first
seeds

5000 B.C.

Corn's Mysterious Beginnings

Aztec tradition explains that a good-hearted ant carried the first corn kernels to humankind from the underworld. This tale may have a grain of truth in it, for the origin of *Zea mays* is still a subject of fierce debate. The only certainty is that botanists disagree about exactly how it could have evolved. The problem with maize, as corn is also called, is that unlike most grains, there are no undisputed wild relatives from which it springs. A wild grass called teosinte will freely interbreed with maize, but these two plants differ in ways that make proof of ancestry difficult. (Some scientists even suggest that teosinte evolved from maize.) Maize as it exists today—and in its earliest remains from more than 7,000 years ago—is helpless in the wild. The kernels are crowded too closely together to sprout successfully without horticultural help, even if they did manage to escape their enveloping husks.

So how did it first appear? Why is there no evidence of a wild relative? The story of its underground origin has an appeal. What seems likely is that maize was already domesticated in Mexico by 5000 B.C., perhaps owing its existence to an extinct wild ancestor or to a brief and intense period of hybridization with teosinte. It may have sprung up independently in South America, where maize was domesticated and revered by 2000 B.C.

Apart from its questionable origins, maize is indisputably a versatile, varied, and prolific crop upon which American civilization grew and prospered. More productive than wheat, it can be eaten young as a vegetable or left to mature and be ground into a nutritious flour. And even the very earliest races of American farmers had discovered the delights of popcorn. A Mayan myth suggests the status of maize in the New World: Humankind, it is said, only succeeded when the gods molded men and women out of a dough made from maize.

4000 B.C.

Peruvian Potatoes

Ten thousand years before a potato first plunged into boiling oil, *Solanum tuberosum* constituted part of the Peruvian diet. Sifting through the debris of caves high in the Andes, archaeologists have found the remains of potatoes dating from approximately 8000 B.C. In those days, potato eating was risky business. The many wild species (more than 200 occur between Colorado and Chile) tended to be bitter with toxic alkaloids. In seeking varieties without this drawback, early gatherers gradually established a range of species safe for eating in quantity. By 4000 B.C., farmers in the highlands of what is now Peru and Bolivia were cultivating potatoes, squash, and lima beans, supplementing their protein intake with the flesh of domesticated guinea pigs. Dried and preserved as *chuño*, potatoes served as a year-round staple for these early mountain farmers.

Potatoes in those days were not the white and bland standbys of today's fast-food industry. Peruvian markets still amaze North American visitors with their rainbow of tubers—blue, black, gold, even spotted and striped—testimony to a diversity that has sustained indigenous farmers since the dawn of agriculture.

3500 B.C.

Farming Spreads throughout Europe

It is difficult to imagine Europe without its dense patchwork of intensively farmed fields. But farming did not become widespread throughout the continent until several millennia after agriculture had transformed society in the Middle East. Some historians think farming spread by waves of colonization from Greece to

3000 B.C.

The Revolutionary Plow

The plow was at first only a modest success. In its simplest form, it was merely the limb of a tree with a branch protruding at such an angle that its sharpened point tore into the ground when pulled through a field. Two people were required to operate it: one to pull, one to steer. At some point in the fourth millennium B.C., however, farmers in the Near East conceived of a purpose for their cattle besides milk and meat. By hitching a rope around the horns of an ox or cow and fastening the other end to their plow, they halved the human power needed to plow and significantly increased their traction. By 3000 B.C., farmers were breaking the sod of Egypt and Mesopotamia by attaching two beasts at the neck with a wooden yoke. There would not be another such revolution in agriculture for nearly 5,000 years.

France; others believe that the resident hunter-gatherer people of Europe learned from their gardening neighbors. Whatever the reason, farming was an idea whose time had come. It took less than 300 years for agricultural settlements to spread from eastern Europe to Belgium. By 4000 B.C., most of central Europe was plowing the land; 500 years later, even Britain and Scandinavia had succumbed to the agricultural way of life.

Early Europeans grew wheat, barley, peas, and beans. They lived in solid wooden houses, and it wasn't long before they began to grow hedges to separate their fields. Cattle, pigs, and sheep supplemented their diets and fertilized their fields. When the use of the plow became widespread in about 2500 B.C., the face of European farming took on a familiar look, one that would remain constant for centuries. The peasant of A.D. 1800 would have known how to subsist on the Stone Age farm.

Words of Conservation

"Mountains exhausted of forests are washed bare by torrents," explained an agricultural document from the reign of the mythical Chinese emperor Shen Nung (reputed to have been the discoverer of tea and the inventor of acupuncture). Even then, the soil of the highlands, loosened by agriculture, was eroding down the slopes and giving the Yellow River its famous hue. And people knew both cause and solution. "To rule the mountain is to rule the river," Shen Nung announced. But the hills continued to erode; then, as now, talking about responsible farming was easier than taking action.

Water Everywhere

Prosperous Egyptians cherished their walled gardens, where the square plots were lined with flowers and shaded by the likes of date palms, fig trees, sycamores, willows, tamarisks, and even pomegranates. Watering these lush, private oases, however, was a never-ending task. Although many householders had pools, the problem was—as always—how to get water to the plants.

At first, Egyptian gardeners transported water in clay pots that were balanced on a yoke on their shoulders. By the time of the New Kingdom (1570–1070 B.C.), though, a simple machine had come to the gardener's aid. The shadoof, or well-sweep, consisted of an upright post with a horizontal beam mounted on a pivot at the top. From one end of the beam hung a bucket; a weight counterbalanced the other end. Up-to-date gardeners of that time simply filled their buckets, then swung the shadoof and emptied the water into the irrigation trenches that crisscrossed their gardens. Rarely portrayed in agricultural scenes, the shadoof seems to have been largely for domestic use—an early item in ancient garden centers.

1500 B.C.

Good Advice from On High

While leading his people away from their years of captivity in Egypt, Moses received divine instruction on the practice of agriculture in the promised land: "Six years thou shalt sow thy field…," God told Moses on Mount Sinai, "but in the seventh year shall be a sabbath of rest unto the land" (Leviticus 25:3–4). This was more than mere respect for the six days spent creating the universe. The sabbatical year of rest served as a fallow period so the soil could replenish its nutrients. In another area, Jewish religious rituals similarly complemented sound agriculture. According to the Talmud, an underground conduit channeled blood from the sacrificial altar to a collecting point outside the city. There, gardeners could purchase the blood as fertilizer. Not all aspects of Jewish agriculture were rooted in religious tradition, however. The Israelites are believed to have learned the invaluable lessons of contour plowing and terracing the steep hills of Palestine from their heathen neighbors and bitter enemies, the Philistines.

1483 B.C.

Hatshepsut's Garden for the Gods

The remarkable Egyptian queen Hatshepsut—when she wasn't busy constructing temples or building industry—recorded how the god Amon instructed her to make a garden big enough for him to walk in. She took his request seriously, sending out an expedition that brought back 32 incense trees—with their roots carefully enclosed in sacks of soil—from the land of Punt (present-day Somalia). The trees grew to a great height, offering the god a shady grove to wander through.

1150 B.C.

Early Flower Fanatic

Of all the royal benefactors of gardening, Egypt's Ramses III was probably the most enthusiastic. An avid importer of trees and flowers, the king also created gardens—"wide places to walk in with all kinds of trees that bear sweet fruit," as he himself described them, "glowing with the flowers of every country, with lotus and papyrus, numberless as the sands." His contributions to temples included 514 gardens and a carefully recorded 19,130,032 bouquets. Ramses's talents for gold mining and his botanical charms were not enough to keep a stray wife from attempting his assassination, but the king escaped unharmed, surviving to sniff another bouquet.

Ancient Fields of the Andes

Long before the Incas ruled the largest American empire, Peruvian growers had developed an intensive farming method that infused the cold plain around Lake Titicaca with astonishing fertility. The idea was simple: Farmers dug a series of parallel canals, using the soil they had dug to make raised fields between the channels. The fields, known as waru waru, were 12 to 30 feet wide, 30 to 300 feet long, and 3 feet high. They remained well drained in wet seasons but had a ready store of water available during droughts. At an elevation of 12,500 feet, where temperatures soar and plunge, these canals created a temperate microclimate. The water absorbed the sun's heat during the day, releasing it at night. At the height of the Inca civilization, 200,000 acres of waru waru were used, representing about 145 million days of construction. Modern experiments have shown why farmers worked so hard at this system; potato yields on reconstructed waru waru have nearly quadrupled conventional harvests.

29

Integrated Pest Poetry

"Where thistle and smartweed lie rotting, Millet grows apace." *The Book of Songs*, one of China's classic texts, is more than exquisite poetry. It offers a vivid portrait of Chinese life, including agriculture. Many of the modern gardener's anxieties and prayerful hopes are caught in verses composed nearly 3,000 years ago:

> *There are no bare patches,*
> *everywhere our crops sprout,*
> *They are firm, they are good,*
> *There is no foxtail, no weeds.*
> *Avaunt, all earwigs and pests,*
> *Do not harm our young crops.*

The Empire of the Garden

The art of gardening grew up quickly. In a mere three or four thousand years, humanity progressed from learning the basis of subsistence agriculture—irrigation, harvesting, and seed collection—to mastering landscape design, grafting, and soil analysis. Whoever created the Hanging Gardens of Babylon had no Ph.D. in horticulture, but today that designer would hold a professorship at any design school. Wherever the Roman farming authority Columella learned his craft, it was not at an agricultural college, yet he cared for the land with a knowledge and love that is rare. The world of 2,000 years ago boasted royal pleasure parks, thriving farms that produced food for all seasons, and even the beginnings of the suburban garden, complete with birdbaths, flowerbeds, and furniture for alfresco dining.

For gardeners in the first millennia B.C. and A.D., as always, some things went wrong. Caterpillars ate the cabbages, torrential rains drowned seedlings, and the sun parched the half-grown crops. And, as always, people muddled through. But even the best gardeners were defenseless against the greater assaults from society itself—the wars, recessions, taxes, repression, and poverty. In Europe, people watched helplessly as their farms failed, their lands eroded, and their civilizations slid into an era that historians have called, with some justice, the Dark Ages.

750 B.C.
Homer describes classical gardens in *The Odyssey*.

563 B.C.
The future Buddha is born in the shade of the Plaksha tree, one more reason Buddhists revere trees.

500 B.C.
Confucius brushes aside the importance of garden design, but the Chinese ignore him, seeking perfect early Feng Shui gardens.

c. 441 B.C.
Sophocles writes *Antigone*.

753 B.C.
Romulus and Remus found Rome.

Nebuchadnezzar II in Mesopotamia has the Hanging Gardens of Babylon built.

600 B.C.

401 B.C.
Xenophon and other Greeks traveling to Persia find lush walled paradise gardens.

399 B.C.
Socrates is accused of corrupting youth and is condemned to death by drinking hemlock.

Greek philosophers enjoy their olive groves and gardens that bloomed immoderately with roses and other flowers.

387 B.C.

250 B.C.

Archimedes explains how the lever works.

221 B.C.

Shih Huang Ti takes power and protects his empire from the Huns by building the Great Wall of China.

160 B.C.

Roman senator Marcus Porcius Cato recommends plowing and manuring to his constituents.

After conquering Gaul, Julius Caesar conquers Britain.

54 B.C.

c. **200** B.C.

The Hindu text the Bhagavad Gita is written.

85 B.C.

Chinese farmers use simple machines to plant seeds.

300 B.C.

The Father of Botany, Theophrastus, recommends planting seeds and manuring.

235 B.C.

Syracuse's ruler Hieron II creates a floating garden, foreshadowing the popularity of cruise ships.

36 B.C.

Marcus Terentius Varro writes 600 books, including *On Agriculture*, in which Varro mourns the dwindling number of small farms.

A.D. 64

Columella advises manuring, crop rotation, and soil tasting.

Rome is nearly destroyed by fire.

A.D. 105

A Chinese imperial court official, Ts'ai Lun, makes paper from hemp, rags, and fishnets.

C. 4 B.C.

Jesus of Nazareth is born.

A.D. 60

Jesus' parables—including one about a barren fig tree—were being written.

Jesus' mustard seed story spreads, inspiring many—and fueling botanical debates.

A.D. 25

Buddhism spreads from China to India.

A.D. 79

Vesuvius erupts; its ash preserves the remains of Pompeiian gardens.

A.D. 100

Pliny the Elder and Pliny the Younger describe and take up topiary in fair Toscana.

A.D. 300

Chinese gardeners control orchard pests with ants.

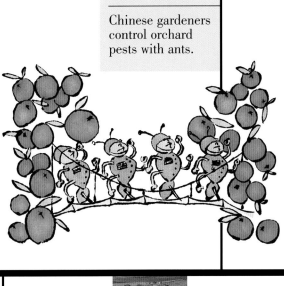

A.D. 400

Chinese poet T'ao Ch'ien plucks petals of popular yellow chrysanthemums.

Saint Patrick travels from England to Ireland to convert the Irish to Christianity.

A.D. 432

A.D. 138

Emperor Hadrian puts on further airs by building a 450-acre garden filled with fountains, pools, sculpture, and imported plants.

A.D. 350

The *Kama Sutra* recommends that women plant kitchen gardens.

A.D. 410

The Goths invade Rome.

A.D. 476

Romans deforest hills, produce less food, and decline.

Homer's Charmed Landscapes

After years of fighting for his life—against monsters, gods, and women—Homer's Odysseus finally reached the safety of a friendly island. Wandering alone in the grand palace of King Alcinous, Odysseus glanced outside and stared in wonder at the beautiful garden, where rows of fruit trees— pears, pomegranates, apples, figs, and olives—stood ready for harvesting. Grapevines, vegetable beds, and flowers completed the idyllic scene. As it turns out, Alcinous was no ordinary gardener. The flowers, Homer tells us, were always in bloom; the fruits and vegetables always ripe for picking. Magic or not, *The Odyssey* gives readers a rare glimpse of Greek gardens in the classical era.

A Living, Growing Roof

The best-known garden in the world, next to Eden, left no trace of its existence. On the basis of breathless accounts by later historians, however, the Hanging Gardens of Babylon are counted among the Seven Wonders of the Ancient World. One story has it that King Nebuchadnezzar II of Mesopotamia constructed these towering gardens on the banks of the Euphrates to please a wife who longed for the mountains of her native Persia. A series of terraces, supported by arches, arose from a massive rectangular base. Walkways and royal chambers stretched beneath the terraces. A huge roof garden topped the structure. According to one account, teams of men worked constantly to pump up water from the river. No one knows what trees and shrubs were planted, but from a distance, the amazing garden must have resembled a lush, green pyramid.

Gardens of Contemplation

563 B.C.

Queen Māyā, knowing she was about to give birth, saw the Plaksha tree bowing its branches in reverence to her. Under its shelter, she gave birth painlessly to the infant Siddhārtha Gautama. Years later Prince Gautama, in search of a spiritual life, received his Great Enlightenment while sitting under a bo tree, the sacred fig of India. Since then, tree-shaded gardens have been central to the meditative Buddhist way of life. Both lifestyle and ideal gardens are described by scriptures with the evocative formula: "not too noisy by day, perfectly quiet by night, removed from disturbance and crowds, a place of retreat and lonely contemplation."

Early Feng Shui

500 B.C.

It is said that Confucius, distracted from more-important studies by a pupil who wanted his views on gardening, responded irritably, "As for gardens, leave such things to gardeners." Although the sage's testy reply discouraged scholars from pursuing horticulture, the Chinese took garden design far beyond the logic of Confucius. Gardening became a spiritual exercise, harmonizing the elements of nature with the human soul in an artful composition of water, rocks, and plants.

Garden Paradise

401 B.C.

Paradise began in Persia. The word paradise derives from the Avestan (ancient Persia's language) *pairi*, meaning "around," and *daeza*, meaning "wall." In an arid climate where the lush growth of an irrigated garden was close to many people's ideas of heaven, it is no wonder that the walled oases where Persians grew flowers and fruits became associated with the pleasures of eternity.

The Greek historian Xenophon witnessed the formal beauty of Persian gardens. Symmetrical plots shaded by cypresses, palms, or pomegranates flanked ornamental waterways. Cyrus the Younger, known for his bloody rebellion against the Persian state, surprised Xenophon by claiming to have designed his own royal pleasure garden. On occasion, boasted the down-to-earth general, he even did his own planting.

Rhodes by Any Other Name

Western philosophy was born in the garden. Plato established his Academy (c. 387 B.C.) in an olive grove outside Athens, and he lived in a garden of his own nearby. Aristotle wandered with his pupils through the gardens of the Lyceum, northeast of the city. In a country so bare of trees, gardens were places of refuge from the scorching summer sun. Olives, plane trees, cypresses, myrtles, pomegranates, and laurels helped cool the philosophical mind. The Greeks cultivated violets, narcissi, tulips, crocuses, lilies, daisies, and irises, but none of these was more popular than the rose. Sailors knew they were approaching the island of Rhodes, it is said, because the fragrance of rose blossoms wafted to their ships from beyond the horizon.

An Early Botanical Encyclopedia

When the great philosopher Aristotle died, he left his garden at the Athens Lyceum school to his favorite pupil and close friend, Theophrastus (c. 372–c. 285 B.C.). The younger man inherited all of his master's zest for knowledge of all sorts . Of the 227 treatises Theophrastus is said to have written, nearly all have been lost, but with just one book, Theophrastus stands uncontested as the Father of Botany. His comprehensive *Inquiry into Plants* covers the physical properties of many growing things, from the weight-bearing strength of timber to the use of wild cucumber to cure mange in sheep. The *Inquiry* also includes some practical advice for the Athenian gardener: Sow vetch to keep pests away from radishes, he suggests. For best results, plant your vegetable seeds, rather than just scattering them. He also points out that "manured land gets the start by as much as 20 days of that which has not been manured."

235 B.C.

Garden Cruises

Not content with a garden on his palace grounds, Hieron II of Syracuse ordered for himself a floating garden, "luxuriant with plants of marvelous growth, and watered by lead tiles hidden from sight." The prince's pleasure boat also came equipped with a gymnasium and walkways shaded with ivy and grapevines.

160 B.C.

Roman Manure

"Plan to have a big compost heap," advised Marcus Porcius Cato (234–149 B.C.), a Roman soldier and senator who wrote the first agricultural manual in Latin after retiring to his farm. Cato was an experienced farmer who knew, without the benefit of agricultural science, that legumes such as lupines, beans, and vetch enriched the soil. *On Agriculture* is full of blunt, practical advice. The commanding voice of the old general resounds down through the centuries: "What is the first principle of good agriculture? To plow well. What is the second? To plow again; and the third is to manure."

36 B.C.

On Snails and Olive Oil

What is the best way to keep snails? When should I prune my olives? Where should I locate my manure pit? Whatever the gardening question, Marcus Terentius Varro (116–27 B.C.) had the answer. A man with a voracious appetite for learning, Varro wrote more than 600 books during his long life. He started writing his own *On Agriculture* at age 80, drawing on his knowledge of more than 50 ancient texts. Varro's love of farming shines through his three volumes of practical advice, but not all Romans shared his passion. He sadly observed that the small farms were disappearing, their owners preferring the theaters and circuses of the capital to the toil of their farms.

c. A.D. **60**

The Virtues of Fertilizing

By the end of the first century, the four Gospels of the New Testament would be written down. They contain advice for all people, including the gardener. In preaching on the need for repentance, Jesus of Nazareth told a parable about a man whose fig tree had not borne fruit for three years. The man angrily ordered his gardener to cut it down, but the gardener (who had clearly not been paying much attention to the tree) had a request: "Let it alone this year also, till I shall dig about it, and dung it" (Luke 13:8).

Jesus was pointing out that the unproductive soul will meet destruction. The gardener was merely giving some concise and excellent gardening advice: Aerate and fertilize your soil.

44

c. A.D. **60**

Much Ado about Mustard

Jesus had no intention of setting off a centuries-long feud among botanists when he told his parable of the mustard seed. "The kingdom of heaven is like to a grain of mustard seed," he said, "which a man took, and sowed in his field." This tiny seed grew to "the greatest among herbs," so sturdy that birds could sit in it. But what exactly did Jesus mean by "mustard," asked botanists. Most favored ordinary black mustard (*Brassica nigra*), which has a small seed and grows 3 to 4 feet high. Others argued vigorously for the related *Sinapsis alba*, or white mustard. The biblical plant wasn't a mustard at all, claimed a vocal minority, but a weedy bush—the *Salvadora persica*—which grows in the Holy Land. Nonsense; why would anyone sow a weed in his garden, fired back the majority. Perhaps it was actually the American pokeberry, suggested one botanist, who was dismissed as "a vain charlatan" by another indignant scholar. Like the seed in the story, this fine point of botany had grown well beyond anyone's imaginings.

45

A.D. 64

Columella's Soil Tea

"A cabbage ought to be transplanted when it consists of six leaves, provided that its root is smeared with liquid manure and wrapped up in three bands of seaweed." With such attention to detail, it is no wonder that Lucius Junius Columella was revered for his gardening wisdom well into the seventeenth century. His 12-part treatise on agriculture, *Res rustica*, advised Romans on all aspects of rural life, from choosing their land and organizing their buildings to yoking oxen and storing eggs. Cultivating the land, Columella believed, was a noble calling. Roman farms were failing because landowners were ignorant of sound farming techniques. A fervent advocate of crop rotation, contour plowing, and regular manuring, Columella took his passion to extremes that would daunt most modern gardeners: Check the quality of your soil, he suggested, by steeping it in water and tasting the strained liquid for sweetness.

A.D. 79

Utility and Beauty under Ash

The cloud of volcanic ash that blanketed Pompeii in A.D. 79 would preserve for centuries the quiet life of middle-class Roman gardeners. Houses that would have been built over or pulled down in the normal passage of time would instead emerge from the earth during later excavations, providing a wealth of information about the ordinary householder. Even some of the larger plants that were growing the day Mount Vesuvius erupted have rematerialized; archaeologists have been able to make plaster casts of plants buried in volcanic ash, so we can see what Pompeiian plants looked like.

A typical Pompeiian garden was a rectangular courtyard near the center of the house, perhaps visible from the street through an open vestibule. Where space was not an issue, covered walkways occupied all four sides. Their roofs, supported by columns, sloped inward to collect precious rainwater in an underground cistern. The garden would often include an ornamental pool and religious or decorative statuary—possibly of Venus (the protector of gardens), a chubby child, or even the family dog. Stone slabs sometimes served as built-in couches for outside dining.

Roman gardeners loved their flowers. Roses, madonna lilies, poppies, daisies, narcissi, and violets were favorites. Ivy and grapevines trailed over trellises and pergolas. Shrubs might have included bay, lavender, rosemary, juniper, acanthus, and viburnum. Most of these plants served medicinal purposes, so the Roman garden doubled as the bathroom medicine cabinet.

47

Tuscan Topiary

No one knows exactly when a fanciful gardener first took a pair of shears and cut a shrub into the shape of a pyramid, a sailing ship, or an eagle, but the art of topiary has thrived at least since the Roman Empire. Pliny the Elder, in his massive *Natural History*, describes the technique as if it were a novelty. His nephew (also named Pliny), a wealthy Roman official with an unrivaled appetite for writing letters, put the art into practice. Writing to a Roman friend who wonders why he should want a villa in faraway Tuscany, the younger Pliny describes his magnificent estate. A sloping bank leads down from his terrace, he says, and on both sides are shrubs cut into the shapes of animals facing each other. Below is a walkway with more sculpted bushes, and then a stretch of tranquil meadow. Besides all this, Pliny points out, there's no need to dress in the country, because no one ever comes to visit! In Pliny's day, tourism had yet to invade Tuscany.

An Over-the-Top Emperor

One of Rome's most energetic and extravagant rulers, the emperor Hadrian did nothing in moderation. When he built a wall, he stretched it from coast to coast across Britain. And when he turned his attention to gardens, he created a fantastic palace complex east of Rome, the buildings and grounds covering 450 acres. No one knows for certain just what the gardens at Hadrian's villa looked like. What remains among the pillaged ruins suggests a fantastic landscape of marble statuary, fountains, and reflecting pools. Doubtless, Hadrian took trophies of his conquests, importing exotic shrubs and flowers from throughout his far-flung empire. His pleasure palace proved the envy and inspiration for would-be emperors of the Renaissance, when noble gardeners began imitating the pretensions of ancient Rome with their own extravagant landscapes.

Ant Patrol

Long before anyone had come up with the term "Integrated Pest Management," Chinese gardeners were practicing pest control based on sound observation. One inventive technique was to establish colonies of predatory ants in citrus orchards. And to make life easier for their guests, the gardeners constructed little bridges of bamboo so that the ants could run from tree to tree, devouring caterpillars and beetles.

51

A.D. 300

A.D. 350

Love among the Mustard Plants

"A virtuous woman, who has affection for her husband, should act in conformity with his wishes as if he were a divine being." Better known for its instructions regarding a woman's erotic duties, the *Kama Sutra* also directs the housewife of India's Gupta period (320–550) to keep a garden. "She should surround the house with a garden. In the garden, she should plant beds of green vegetables, bunches of the sugarcane, and clumps of the fig tree, the mustard plant, the parsley plant, the fennel plant." Instructions for a kitchen garden seems unusual in a manual devoted to the art of love, but it may be assumed that the couple in question would work up an appetite from other activities described in the text.

Elixir of Youth

The fall chrysanthemums have lovely colors
I pluck the petals that are wet with dew.

One of China's greatest poets, T'ao Ch'ien, did not pick chrysanthemums solely for aesthetic purposes. He goes on to describe dropping the petals in wine, an infusion widely believed to increase longevity. By T'ao's time, the chrysanthemum was a long-established garden flower, referred to in classic texts dating back to 1000 B.C. For centuries, however, all chrysanthemums were yellow. Only during the T'ang dynasty (618–902) did Chinese horticulturists develop a white variety.

A.D. 476

Dawning of the Dark Ages

Rome was so confident of its power to conquer new territory and bring more land into cultivation that it neglected the fields in its own backyard. From as early as 200 B.C., the empire failed to grow enough grain for its own population, and the situation in outlying provinces deteriorated during the centuries of imperial rule. Topsoil streamed off the deforested hillsides. Absentee landlords abandoned their huge estates to ignorant or uncaring tenants. The land produced less and less food, and the populations of the cities dwindled. Many other factors played a part, but bad farming practices doubtless helped to plunge Europe into the Dark Ages.

The Dark Ages, historians have pointed out, is a misleading name for an era. Even in that turbulent period—stretching roughly from the sixth to the thirteenth centuries—there were years of tranquility and sanity, when people in Europe lived long, happy lives without the fear of sudden disruption. And there was gardening, both for pleasure and for food. Although there are few written descriptions of gardens during the Dark Ages, we know that even in those hard times, people did not abandon the earth. Monasteries blossomed with carefully tended flowers and herbs. Peasants hoed their leeks, cabbages, and beans with the same attention and affection that people have shown in any era. In the words of a twelfth-century German monk, "A delightful garden should have violets and white roses, lilies, fruit trees, green grass, and a running stream." That definition would satisfy most modern gardeners.

Beyond the confines of Europe, the world was far from dark. The new faith of Islam introduced the exquisite "paradise" gardens of Persia to conquered lands ranging from Spain to the Indian subcontinent. The exuberant landscape art of China and the meticulous miniatures of Japan spoke of enlightened philosophies. Asia's gardens expressed a unity with the natural world, an environmental consciousness that the West would not embrace for many centuries.

630

Chinese scholar Hiuen Tsang writes of India's lush fruits, spices, and grains—and a curious lack of garlic and onions.

570

Muhammad is born.

700

Hohokam people irrigate the American Southwest with an intricate system of canals.

640

The windmill is invented in Persia.

715

The Moors defeat the Visigoths, conquering most of Spain.

530

Benedictine monks support themselves with farms, physic gardens, vineyards, and breweries in Italy.

618

The T'ang dynasty begins ruling China.

c. 587

Buddhism starts to spread throughout Japan.

637

Islamic Crusaders spread garden practices and the Koran's wisdom throughout Europe, the Middle East, Asia, and Africa.

814

Charlemagne dictates what gardeners should plant.

925

Roses are used for healing and mischief but are rarely grown merely for their beauty.

1000

Moors create shady gardens and sunken beds; nobles can walk among the treetops.

Leif Eriksson lands on the northeastern coast of North America and names it Vinland.

840

A German monk writes garden poetry and "summons back the worms."

900

Tofu becomes a dietary staple in China.

970

Gardens perk up solemn English cathedrals.

800

Chinese gardeners imitate wild elements, flower collectors spend wildly, and poet Po Chü-i writes it all down.

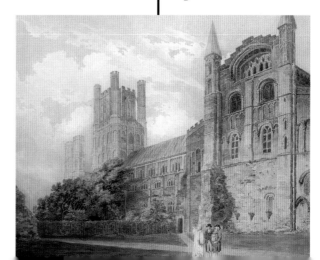

1040

Macbeth becomes king of Scotland after murdering King Duncan.

1080

In Seville, the sultan's gardener "confounds" slugs with ashes.

1141

Bingen's Benedictine abbess Hildegard catalogs plants and writes of God as the force of "greenness."

1050

Sakuteiki describes how Japanese gardeners create miniature ecosystems.

1020

The *Tale of Genji* chronicles the Japanese blossom fetish.

1054

The Church formally splits into two branches, Orthodox and Roman.

Theodora rules the Byzantine empire.

1066

The Normans win the Battle of Hastings, defeating Saxon rule of England; William the Conqueror ascends to the throne.

1099

Jerusalem is taken in the First Crusade.

1100

Chinese Emperor Hui Tsung creates symbolic topography—then goes bankrupt.

1207

Persian poet and Sufi mystic Jalāl al-Dīn Rūmī is born; he will write the *Masnavi,* a mystical Sufi epic.

1271

Marco Polo begins his travels to China.

1260

Early lawn fetishes take root in Germany, writes Albertus Magnus.

1285

Alessandro di Spina invents eyeglasses.

1200

Alexander Neckam recommends companion planting to Londoners.

1215

Mongol emperor Genghis Khan conquers China.

1250

Abbess Euphemia and other British women sow, weed, and harvest.

60

Franziskaner.

The Monastic Tradition

Since the earliest days of Christianity, devout hermits had cultivated patches of land to keep themselves alive. In 530, an Italian nobleman named Benedict, who had rejected the worldly life, established a holy order of monks on Monte Cassino. The self-supporting Benedictines (and other orders that later spread throughout Europe) became skilled and industrious gardeners, establishing a monastic tradition that has continued into the twenty-first century. Apart from growing the staple vegetables—beans, peas, cabbages, and onions—the monks kept livestock, bred fish, made honey and cheese, manufactured medicines from their "physic gardens," and brewed an intemperate quantity of beer and wine.

630

A Chinese Monk in India

Journeying through India in search of holy texts, the Chinese Buddhist Hiuen Tsang left a remarkable record of his pilgrimage, including observations on the produce and gardening practices of his hosts. "It would be difficult to enumerate all the kinds of fruit," he wrote, adding that oranges and pomegranates grew everywhere. Rice and wheat were plentiful, along with ginger, mustard, melons, and pumpkins. He was struck, however, by the relative scarcity of onions and garlic. "If anyone uses them for food," he explained, "they are expelled beyond the walls of the town."

637

Paradises on Earth

The Islamic conquerors who burst into the Persian capital of Ctesiphon in 637 were themselves conquered by the serene beauty of the gardens they discovered there. These enclosed sanctuaries of shade trees and artificial watercourses must have reminded the new rulers of the beautiful afterlife promised to them in their own sacred writings. According to the Koran, Islam's holy book, "those who believe and do deeds of righteousness" will live forever in the gardens of paradise. The righteous will find there "neither sun nor bitter cold," but will enjoy for eternity "shades and fountains and such fruits as their hearts desire." Waters flow beneath paradise, and four rivers flow continuously over the surface: rivers of water, milk, wine, and honey. In the mortal world—parched and sun-baked—images such as these were visions of true paradise.

An Oasis in Arizona

While peasants in Europe struggled to produce enough cabbages and beans to survive, a people in southwestern North America were making the desert bloom. These people, the Hohokam, as they came to be known, lived in the area where Phoenix now sits. Settling in this arid land around the first century A.D., the Hohokam developed a vibrant economy based on a sophisticated system of agriculture. Like their southwestern neighbors, the Hohokam grew maize, beans, and squash, but with only 7½ inches of rain a year, the prospect of successful harvests was remote without irrigation. By 700, they were bringing water from the Salt River to their villages by a complex network of canals.

At least 500 miles of main canals—some of them 75 feet wide—led to irrigation ditches that watered fields. For 700 years, their culture prospered. Then, quite suddenly, it collapsed. By 1400 the canals were in disrepair, the villages in ruins. Disease, warfare, climate change, and environmental mismanagement are all possible causes of their downfall. Subsequent inhabitants of the region knew their predecessors only by their evocative name, Hohokam, or "those who have vanished."

The Islamic invaders enthusiastically mastered the art of Persian gardening and carried it with them on their wildfirelike conquests—west across northern Africa and into Spain, and east to India—planting garden paradises of their own wherever they settled. Some of history's noblest gardens would later emerge as a result of this religious crusade, from the Alhambra palace in Spain to the majestic Taj Mahal memorial in India. Shaded by fruit-bearing trees and often divided by four channels of flowing water (symbolizing the four rivers of paradise), these Islamic gardens were oases for the spirit. The devout gardener, however, would remember with humility the words of the Koran: "There would be no gardens in this world or rivers if it were not for the Gardens and Rivers of Paradise."

64

On Wilderness Gardens and Peonies

According to Chinese gardening tradition, art should imitate nature. Even in the smallest urban space, a gardener could meticulously arrange rocks, plants, and water to simulate the effect of wilderness. The poet Po Chü-i (772–846) wrote affectionately of his garden: a pool with lotus blossoms, a grove of bamboos, a path of white stones. But Chinese gardening was not all poetry and purity. Po Chü-i lived at a time when collectors were willing to spend small fortunes for the brilliant red blossoms of the mouton, or tree peony. In one poem, Po Chü-i commented wryly on the peony mania of his countrymen. Plants with many blossoms commanded inflated prices, he observed, and the poet ruefully concluded:

> *A cluster of deep-red flowers*
> *Would pay the taxes of ten poor houses.*

Start Gardening: It's the Law

Charlemagne—king of the Franks from 768 to 800, emperor until his death in 814—brought some old-fashioned Roman order back to the political chaos of the Dark Ages. As sole ruler of much of continental Europe, he issued hundreds of laws on subjects ranging from local government to education. His decree concerning towns included a list of 73 flowers and vegetables and 16 fruit and nut trees that should be planted in every city in the empire. It is hard to believe that everyone complied with this order. However, a monastery garden design that was created shortly after Charlemagne's death showed what a useful garden was thought to contain. The design included two gardens: one for vegetables, one for medicine. The monks' cemetery was landscaped with fruit and nut trees, and it doubled as an orchard. In the kitchen garden, next to the poultry house, were 18 beds housing many old friends, such as onions, celery, parsley, parsnips, radishes, carrots, and beets, and a few crops that may surprise the twenty-first-century gardener: black cumin, poppy, and coriander. The "physic" garden, conveniently next to the infirmary, contained 16 species, including roses, lilies, mint, rosemary, fennel, sage, and flag iris—all ingredients from Charlemagne's list of must-haves.

Walahfrid's Little Garden

A shaft of light fell on the gardens of medieval Europe, thanks to a German monk named Walahfrid Strabo. While abbot of Reichenau, "Walahfrid the Squint-Eyed," as he called himself, composed a charming Latin poem on the delights of gardening and the uses of garden plants. His *Hortulus,* or *The Little Garden,* opens with a familiar gardening scene: The plot he intends to cultivate is choked with weeds. Walahfrid relishes manual labor, though. Hacking at the hard earth with a mattock, he tears out the nettles by their roots, "summoning back the worms," as he put it. There follows a list of 23 plants and a summary of their household uses. Gourds serve as wine flasks; fennel cures a cough; iris root, when dried and crushed, will starch linen; celery seed aids digestion; and catmint restores the skin and hair. But the power of Strabo's poem is not so much in his prescriptions—there are other lists more complete—as in the joy he finds in the gardener's simplest tasks. He creates raised beds with planks, and he lovingly waters each of his seedlings drop by drop. And when he writes of lilies and roses, the passion of his affection for growing things speaks to the gardener 12 centuries later like the voice of an old friend.

66

The All-Purpose Rose

A rose was not always a rose—at least not as we know it today. In the modern world, roses are grown as garden ornaments, but in Europe after the fall of Rome, roses were also plants of medical and mystical qualities. There were few tenth-century gardeners who had the luxury of growing flowers simply for their beauty. Everything had a purpose, and the rose was one of the most useful of medicinal plants.

An Anglo-Saxon herbalist named Bald (c. 925), for instance, gave a recipe for curing a sore mouth: rose petals and peppercorns, crushed and infused in hot water as a drink. Roses could be used for mischief, as well. If you harbored secret urges to blight a fruit tree—according to a twelfth-century manuscript—simply combine powdered rose petals, mustard seeds, and the magic ingredient: woodpecker fat. (Then you could hang this concoction on your neighbors' fruit trees and watch their confounded reactions.) St. Benedict found yet another disturbing use for the rose: Because the flower symbolized the blood of Christ, this ascetic monk drew his own blood by tearing his flesh with its thorns.

925 |

970

Flowers at an Abbey

The Isle of Ely was a natural haven in medieval Britain. A 7-mile-long shoulder of rock rising above the swampy fenland north of Cambridge, Ely had provided sure footing for monastic settlements since the seventh century. It was here that Brithnod, Abbot of Ely, planted gardens and orchards in the grounds of his newly con-

structed Benedictine monastery. These, according to a contemporary chronicler, "added much to the commodiousness and the beauty of the place." Drained in the seventeenth century, the fens became dry land, and Ely, an island in name only. Today Ely's majestic cathedral towers above a sea of rich, black earth. The market gardens of this fertile plain—if lacking in beauty—still serve to feed the populace.

Moorish Gardens in Spain

When the Islamic Moors conquered and occupied Spain, they brought with them their love of shady gardens. According to one writer of the era, "The foliage of the garden prevents the sun seeing the ground; and the breeze, blowing day and night over the garden, is loaded with scents." Even more exotic to the European traveler was the Moorish taste for sunken beds, which lowered flowers and shrubs so that their tops would be level with the paths. Eleventh-century gardeners at the Alcázar in Seville planted their orange trees in beds recessed 15 feet below the walkways, letting visitors pass like birds among the scented, flowering upper branches.

1020

Connoisseurs of Blossom

For centuries, Japanese nobles had taken an almost erotic pleasure in flowering trees, particularly cherry and plum trees. Women, it was said, would coordinate their kimonos with the orchards they were to visit. This passion for blossoms is described at its height in the world's oldest novel, the *Tale of Genji*, a long and exquisitely detailed look at life in the Heian court by Lady Murasaki Shikibu. In one scene, an April boating party drifts on a landscaped lake. "Here and there in the distance the topmost boughs of an orchard showed above the mist, so heavily laden with blossom that it looked as though a bright carpet were spread in midair."

The Request of the Stone

Europeans traditionally resorted to rock gardens only when removing stones from their land was too much work. The Japanese, on the other hand, went to considerable lengths to find the perfect stones and place them in their gardens. Then the garden would take shape, "following the request of the stone." The art of gardening with stone and water is carefully explained in *Sakuteiki*, written by a nobleman of the Heian court. This famous manual explains how to make cliffs, beaches, waterfalls (eight kinds), and islands (ten kinds). The aim is a delicate recreation of natural scenery. Flowers and vegetables have no place there, but trees are important. Pines and willows are specified for islands. On the forest island, for instance, "trees should have dense foliage, but the lower part of the trunks should be rather clear of branches." Stones, grass, and sand—thoughtfully distributed beneath the trees—create a landscape in miniature.

1080

Jihad against the Slugs

Spain, invaded by the Islamic Moors in 711, was a bright pool of enlightenment during Europe's Dark Ages. And Arabic gardeners from Spain were the leading horticulturists on the continent. In his *Book of Agriculture*, Ibn Bassal, the chief botanist and gardener for the sultan of Seville, wrote about soil, manure, grafting, pruning, and irrigation. His list of garden plants includes many flowers, indicating that—in Spain, at least—people were gardening for the sheer beauty of it. Throughout history, though, even the greatest gardeners have had to cope with slugs. Here is Ibn Bassal's plan of attack: "Form your beds, strew on them an inch of ashes from the Public Baths, then lay on your manure and sow the seeds: thus the animal mentioned, on leaving the earth in search of the plants, will meet with the ashes and retire confounded."

1100

An Imperial Gardener's Fatal Passion

Emperor Hui Tsung (1082–1135), a skilled artist and gardener, had no male heirs. Consulting his "wind and water" experts, the 26-year-old emperor learned that his land at Kaifeng was too flat. The prescription was simple: Build a fantastic royal garden, complete with an artificial mountain range. Hui Tsung set about this task with the abandon of a man with all the wealth of China at his disposal. Simple flowers and vegetables gave way to orchards and forests, and then to an artfully constructed peak 225 feet high. It was a world in miniature, and the emperor delighted in wandering there. To no one's surprise, he had a son.

But Hui Tsung's preoccupation with gardening helped bring about the fall of the Northern Sung dynasty. Riddled with governmental corruption and completely bankrupt by the expense of its emperor's mountainous folly, China was unable to fight off threats from abroad. In 1126, Juchen tribesmen invaded Kaifeng, the capital. Its inhabitants desperately scrambled to the top of their emperor's beloved mountain, but, fertility symbol or not, the mountain offered no protection from the invaders. Hui Tsung was taken prisoner and died a captive in unlandscaped Manchuria.

The Greenness of God

When she was 42 years old and head of a Benedictine convent, Hildegard von Bingen (1098–1179) was suffused with the spirit of God. "A blinding light of exceptional brilliance flowed through my entire brain," she wrote. "And so it kindled my whole heart and breast like a flame." She devoted the rest of her life to prophetic and scientific writings, musical compositions, and preaching. Her *Physica*, or *Natural History*, includes a descriptive catalog of over 200 plants.

While modern science has cast doubt on some of Hildegard's medical knowledge—eating figs, she claimed, makes a healthy person avaricious—her reputation as a spiritual ecologist has recently blossomed. Hildegard's unique concept of *viriditas*, or greenness, is central to her view of God's purpose. Greenness is the life-giving love of God, bringing health and creativity to the withered world. "In the beginning all creatures were green and vital," Hildegard wrote, and she believed that faith in God would revitalize that life, for the greenness is in God himself. Hildegard had visions in which God spoke to her directly. In one vision he told her, "I am the breeze that nurtures all things green. I encourage blossoms to flourish with ripening fruits." How would this devout German nun respond to her reincarnation, nearly 900 years after her death, as the patron saint of ecofeminism?

76

Companion Plants of England

Young Alexander Neckam, riding into London in 1178, was delighted by the flowers and trees of the sprawling gardens in the prosperous western suburbs. Later he wrote a revered encyclopedia, *De naturis rerum*, identifying the shrubs, flowers, and vegetables that were grown in England (among them the pomegranate, which presumably wintered indoors). Neckam recommended a variety of flowers for gardeners, including the popular roses, lilies, violets, and heliotropes. But medieval gardens generally served a practical purpose as well as a decorative one. Onions, leeks, garlic, beets, and lettuces bedded down alongside the flowers.

1200

Title IX in the Garden

Gardening was an equal-opportunity employer in the Middle Ages. As paintings and documents attest, it was quite acceptable for a woman to pull up her skirts and dig the earth. One of the most successful female gardeners in Britain was Euphemia, Benedictine Abbess of Wherwell, who made her abbey a place of singular beauty. According to a chronicler, "She made gardens and vineyards and shrubberies in places that were formerly useless and barren, and which now became both serviceable and pleasant."

1260

Lawns before Lawn Mowers

"Nothing refreshes the sight so much as fine short grass," wrote the German monk Albertus Magnus in *On Vegetables and Plants.* He goes on to give precise instructions for creating a lawn. First dig up all roots, level the site, and pour boiling water over the whole area to kill any remaining weeds. Then lay down turf of meadow grass and beat the whole plot flat with wooden mallets until the grass is scarcely visible. After a while, says Albertus, a lawn of new young grass will spring up "like a green cloth."

chapter four

Renaissance in the Garden

For centuries, the great estates and villas of the Roman Empire lay in ruins, their gardens gone wild, their creators' knowledge lost or neglected. Only monks and peasants kept the flame of gardening alive. But after nearly 1,000 years, the winds of a new era fanned that flame into a fierce heat. New trade, new technology, new ideas, and finally, new worlds brought a renaissance to the European garden.

Nobles began to create landscaped empires in hedges, lawns, and colorful new flowers from Asia and the Americas. On a lesser scale—in the vegetable patch and cottage flowerbed—the garden was equally vibrant. Kitchen gardeners experimented with corn and new varieties of beans, scorched themselves on peppers, prodded suspiciously at the tomato, and wondered if the rumors they'd heard about the humble sweet potato—and its aphrodisiacal effects—were really true. Tulips, hyacinths, and crocuses added new accents to their flowerbeds, while above these eastern imports nodded the flashy yellow head of America's sunflower.

An important ingredient in the garden renaissance was not a plant but a technology: printing. Early books off the printing press included gardening manuals and treatises. Printing quickly let the patrician learn how to landscape his terraces and the house-holder how to manure his lettuces. It also spawned a new breed: the armchair gardener, whose descendents still dream of ever-taller sunflowers and heavier pumpkins.

1305

Pietro de Crescenzi's lofty garden design book is hand-printed and distributed.

1375

The Alhambra is built, with symmetrical gardens portraying the Koran's vision of creation.

1387

Peony roots become a culinary fad in Europe.

1348

The Black Death spreads from Constantinople through western Europe, killing as much as half the population in some regions.

1350

"The Parisian Householder" recommends that his bride suffocate ants with wet sawdust.

1392

During the Muromachi period, wealthy Japanese gardeners compete fiercely.

1431

In Rouen, France, Joan of Arc is burned at the stake.

1438

The Hundred Years' War, between France and England, begins.

1450

The first English gardening how-to book is published by John the Gardiner.

c. 1450

Johannes Gutenberg invents the printing press.

1493

Beans, chiles, corn, and sweet potatoes travel from the Americas to Europe with Christopher Columbus.

1499

Vasco da Gama returns to Portugal after successfully sailing to India.

1452

Leone Battista Alberti publishes a landscaping guide and recommends Italian country villas.

1462

Ivan the Great—often called the founder of the Russian state—begins to rule Russia.

1510

Hiëronymus Bosch completes his *Garden of Earthly Delights*.

American sunflowers reach Europe; they become a major oilseed crop in some countries, but in others, they are food for the birds.

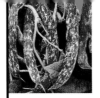

1530

Mexican beans brought to Spain by Cortés reach Italian commoners, broadening the Italian diet.

1539

Cucumbers hitchhike west across the Atlantic; Hernando de Soto finds them in Florida.

1519

Aztecs plant rooftop and floating lake gardens, and make extreme sacrifices to rain and corn gods.

1532

Niccolò Machiavelli's *The Prince* is published.

1550

The potato reaches Spain, but it takes centuries to become fashionable.

1528

Hernán Cortés carries American cocoa, beans, and vanilla beans to Europe after conquering Aztecs in Mexico.

1517

Martin Luther nails his "95 Theses" to the door of a church in Wittenberg and begins the Protestant Reformation in Germany.

1535

Francisco Pizarro conquers Aztecs in Peru.

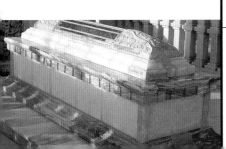

1526

Afghani prince Zahir-ud-din Muhammad, or Babur, conquers India, borrows Indian garden designs, and replants war-ravaged cities.

1554

An Austrian diplomat carries tulip bulbs home from Constantinople and presents them to Dutch botanist Carolus Clusius.

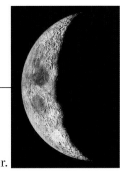

1557

Elizabethan poet Thomas Tusser describes weeds and seeds—in dactylic tetrameter.

1577

Thomas Hill constructs straw cold-frames and writes *The Gardener's Labyrinth.*

1603

Richard Gardiner writes a manual on kitchen garden-ing and sells seeds with zeal.

1559

Pope Paul IV cooks up his *Index librorum prohibitorum,* enforced by the Roman Inquisition. The *Index* will eventually forbid the reading of such works as the Talmud and such authors as Flaubert, Kant, Marx, and Voltaire.

1597

Tomatoes are introduced to England and are met with much disdain and suspicion.

1574

Europeans exclaim that the new sunflower looks "marveilous faire."

1556

Constantinople's Ogier Ghislain de Busbecq describes the tulip, still a stranger to Europe's gardens.

1305

Gardens on a Grand Scale

Italy was the first country to rediscover the learning of ancient Greece and Rome. And the Renaissance, as this enlightening movement became known, swept the art of gardening along with it. In Italy, Pietro de Crescenzi composed a major work—almost entirely borrowed from earlier writers—on garden design. His *Liber ruralium commodorum* was not intended for the average onion-growing peasant. Pietro was concerned with the walled and expansive grounds of the nobility, who had the leisure and the laborers to oversee the meadows, aviaries, menageries, topiaries, and fishponds that he prescribed. One of his more exotic ideas called for "a palace with rooms and towers made uniquely from trees." However impractical his plans may seem, Petrus struck a responsive chord among the gardeners of Europe. Many hand-copied versions of *Liber ruralium commodorum* circulated throughout Europe, and with the invention of printing in 1438, it would be among the first manuscripts to go to press. By 1493 there would be printed editions in four languages. The great gardens of the Renaissance owed some of their inspiration to this early work.

c. 1350

Advice to a Bride

A man who referred to himself anonymously as "The Parisian Householder" (*Le Ménagier de Paris*) left one of the clearest accounts of late medieval gardening. Suspecting that his young bride was going to need help with her new domestic responsibilities, he presented her with a book—a complete guide to household management (c. 1350)—that included gardening as one of its main subjects. The Householder advises readers, including his wife, to spread ash on the ground under cabbages to kill caterpillars and to suffocate ants in their holes with wet sawdust. He also suggests using the dried petals of Provence roses to sweeten clothes and hardening-off violets before putting them outside in the spring. The young lady's response to receiving so much unsolicited advice is unrecorded.

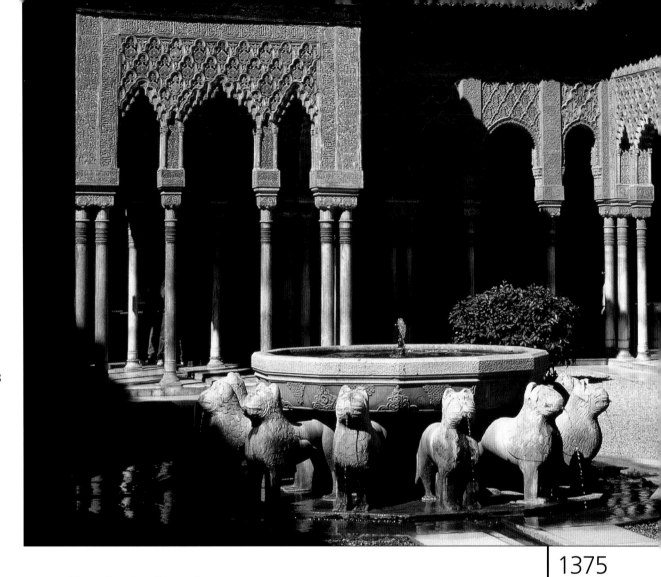

1375

Paradise in Granada

Only a few sites remain that do justice to the greatest gardeners of Europe's Middle Ages. When the Spanish Christians recaptured their land from the Moors in the 1400s, they took few pains to preserve the masterpieces of Islamic landscape gardening. In Granada, however, a famed fortress known as the Alhambra offers a glimpse of the delicate garden art of Spain's former masters. One courtyard in particular, the Patio of the Lions, reveals the Islamic love of symmetry and symbolism. In the center of the court is a great 12-sided fountain, each side

Peony Elixirs

How many peonies does it take to feed a king? England's Richard II (and friends) sat down to 1,200 roasted peony roots in 1387. This was truly a dish fit for a king, as the commoner could not afford to indulge in such a small, slow-growing root. Ordinary people knew the peony primarily as an ingredient in medicines. Since ancient times, the plant had been thought to contain a potent magic. Ancient Greeks believed that peonies could glow in the dark and, in gardens and fields where they grew, would drive away devils. When taken as a "juice" or worn about the neck as an amulet, the peony was an active ingredient in the cure of epileptic convulsions, which were thought of as the devil's particular specialty. Today it's hard to believe that in Renaissance Europe this showy garden flower was valued almost exclusively for its small, fibrous root.

guarded by lions, water trickling from their mouths. Dividing the courtyard into equal quadrants are four channels filled with flowing water. These represent the rivers of creation, a feature of paradise described in the Koran. Today, the Patio of the Lions floor consists of swept, bare sand. In Moorish days it was a scented, shady grove of orange trees, suggesting—in the words of the Koran—"the paradise which the righteous have been promised."

A Matter of Life and Death

At no time in history has gardening been more extravagant and fiercely competitive than in Japan during the Muromachi period (1392–1490). The poor groaned under crippling taxation as the wealthy fought—literally—for flowering cherry or plum trees or for the perfectly shaped rock to landscape their gardens. Temple gardens were routinely plundered for their living treasures. Armies of workers hauled rocks along the roads to noble estates. One fifteenth-century shogun became incensed when he inspected a delivery of plum trees and discovered that a branch was broken. He instantly imprisoned three of the hapless gardeners and set out in pursuit of five knights who had been supervising the delivery. Three of them escaped the country; the remaining two committed suicide.

Cabbages All 'Round

What vegetables did people eat before they had potatoes? The answer, in England at least, is beans, leeks, onions, and cabbages. "John the Gardiner," who wrote the first practical book on gardening in English, pointed out that the cabbage was essential for all ranks, "both to master and to knave." And he took particular care with his onions: Prop up their tops with ash twigs, he suggests. Gardiner describes methods for grafting, pruning, and harvesting, and all in a jingling, rhyming verse that makes his advice easy to remember. In all, he lists 97 plant species. Apart from the absent potato, one notable omission is the carrot, which had not yet arrived from France.

A Tranquil Country Villa

"O blessed country life, how untold are your joys," wrote Leone Battista Alberti (1404–72), mathematician, musician, architect, philosopher, artist—and gardener. Alberti's was the voice most responsible for inspiring Italy to garden with a vigor the country had not seen for 1,000 years. The villa gardens he proposed in *De re aedificatoria* were enclosed by walls for security but built on sloping sites to offer a view. (Look for land with prospects of countryside, city, mountains, and ocean, Alberti advised.) Classically inspired, Alberti's blueprint called for straight rows of trees, symmetrical beds, and closely trimmed hedges, perhaps cut into the shapes of the owner's initials. Even during the Renaissance, a time when the city was the vibrant center of intellectual, artistic, and economic life, people—including Alberti, the ideal "Renaissance man" himself—needed to get away from it all. "There you can escape from the noise and tumult of the city," Alberti wrote of his villa gardens.

Vegetable Immigrants from the New World

93

Spaniards waiting to learn what Christopher Columbus would unpack from the holds of his ships might well have been disappointed to find neither chests of gold nor the sought-after spices of the Far East. But in fact, Columbus had an extremely valuable cargo—although its importance was not immediately apparent. By most people's standards, beans, corn, chiles, and sweet potatoes comprise an unconventional treasure.

In Europe at first, their reception was mixed. European gardeners had beans of their own and so quickly adopted the American species (including scarlet runners and limas) that arrived over the next 50 years. Corn, which would eventually revolutionize agriculture, got off to a slower start. It was "a more convenient food for swine than for man," complained English botanist John Gerard in 1597. Chiles were a hit in Africa and Asia, but at first overwhelmed the flammable palates of northern Europeans. "A very little will set ye throat in such a flame as has ben sometimes deadly," gasped garden writer John Evelyn (1620–1706). Sweet potatoes met with more favor, not just for their surprising burst of sugar, but for their supposed ability to enhance sexual potency: "They comfort, nourish, and strengthen the body procuring bodily lust and that with greediness," wrote one hopeful Englishman.

1493

Beauty and Sacrifice in Mexico

Even the Spanish conquistadors, their minds set on imagined cities of gold, could not help being amazed by the gardens of the Aztecs. "Gardens so wonderful to see and walk in," wrote Bernal Díaz del Castillo, a companion of Cortés, "I was never tired of looking at the diversity of trees, and noting the scent which each one had, and the paths full of roses and flowers." The Spaniards encountered gardens on rooftops, a huge landscaped park equal to any in Europe (according to Cortés himself), and—most remarkably—the *chinampas,* floating gardens that the Aztecs constructed to make use of shallow lakes near their towns. "And of all these wonders that I then beheld," wrote Díaz in a sad postscript, "today all is overthrown and lost, nothing is standing."

The Aztec passion for successful crops led to measures most gardeners would find extreme. To please the corn goddess, Chicomecóatl, each September a young woman was beheaded and skinned. A priest then wore her skin for a week, assuming the identity of the goddess. Late in March, children were sacrificed to the rain god, Tlaloc. Their tears, it was believed, would encourage the god to water the newly sown corn.

Out of the Strong Came Forth Sweetness

Zahir-ud-din Muhammad, or Babur, is known to history as the Mughal prince who swept through the mountains of Afghanistan to conquer India. Although conquering was his destiny (he was a direct descendent of Genghis Khan), gardening was his delight. He beautified his capital city of Kabul with at least 10 garden designs of his own, and even while campaigning abroad, sent instructions to his overseers back home. "The best young trees must be planted there," he wrote of one unfinished project, "lawns arranged, and borders set with sweet herbs and with flowers of beautiful color and scent." A connoisseur of tulips, he compiled a list of 33 varieties.

It is difficult today to reconcile Babur's incessant and bloody military campaigns with his love of fruit trees, flowers, and flowing water. He created gardens wherever he stopped, as if to bring the ruins of conquered cities back to life. If epitaphs are to be believed, Babur is in a garden now. On his grave in Kabul is the simple inscription, "Paradise is forever Babur Padshah's [King Babur's] abode."

Beans from the New World

One species of bean still served up in northeastern Italy has a fancy pedigree. Around the year 1530, Hernán Cortés presented King Charles V of Spain with treasures and handicrafts from the conquered land of Mexico. Among the booty was a sack of dried beans. Charles, in turn, handed the beans to Pope Clement VII. Clearly not a kitchen gardener, Clement gave the beans to a scholar named Pierio Valeriano, who grew them in pots on his rooftop. From this first harvest, as history has it, Valeriano distributed beans to local gardeners—and so a hill of beans became a mountain.

1530 |

1539 |

The Cucumber Discovers America

The traffic in plants across the Atlantic Ocean was by no means a one-way trade affair. By 1494, cucumbers—a favorite of Europe's gardeners since before the Roman Empire—were reported to be growing on the island of Hispaniola, which had been visited by Christopher Columbus in 1492 and settled a year later. How they made the crossing to the North American mainland is unknown, but in 1539 the Spanish explorer Hernando de Soto discovered them growing in Florida's moist soil and pronounced them delicious. Cucumbers might have been the perfect accompaniment to the explorer's green salads, but they were no substitute for the gold he so desperately sought.

1550

Introducing the Potato

The potato arrived in Europe with glowing recommendations. "The potato when boiled is as tender as a cooked chestnut," a Spaniard wrote from the New World in 1536, and others in America confirmed his opinion. The Peruvian tuber received no royal welcome when it reached Spain some time after 1550, but

by 1573, it was being served up to patients at a Seville hospital. Fifty years later the peasants of Ireland had adopted it as a national staple. Two centuries were to pass, however, before this nutritious and versatile vegetable would appear on the middle-class menus of Europe.

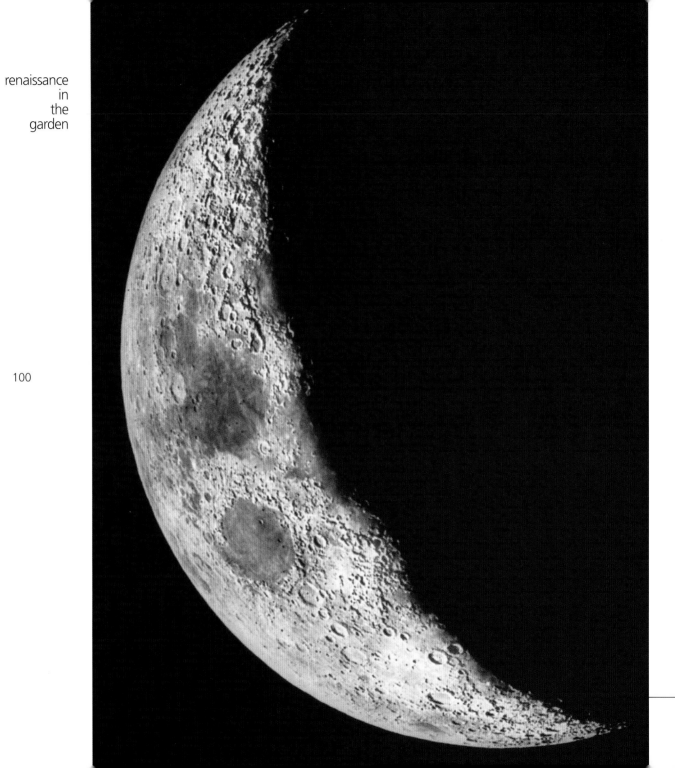

First Word of the Tulip

Writing from Constantinople, Ogier Ghislain de Busbecq enthused about a flower known as the "tulipan." It had "little or no scent," he admitted, "but is admired for its beauty and the variety of its colours." This is the first Europe had heard of the tulip, a flower that would drive gardeners to a state approaching madness early in the next century.

A Garden of Verses

Anyone new to gardening in Elizabethan England would have been wise to consult Thomas Tusser's *Five Hundred Pointes of Good Husbandrie*. Arranged as a monthly schedule of farming tasks, Tusser's book takes the reader through the gardening year, month by month. What should you do in February? Well, to begin with, make sure to spread your manure before you plow in the stubble. Then sow your peas and beans—but wait for the waning moon. All of Tusser's tips are in a bouncy, childlike verse, like this May entry on weeding your wheat (called "corne"):

> *In Maie get a weede hooke, a crotch and a glove,*
> *and weed out such weedes as the corne doth not love.*

Apart from the accidental humor of his style, Tusser provides a comprehensive checklist of Elizabethan agricultural duties: washing sheep, catching moles, storing straw, and scaring birds. Gardeners in Shakespeare's day, we learn, were swapping seeds:

> *One seede for another, to make an exchange,*
> *with fellowlie neighbourhood seemeth not strange.*

Tusser's *Good Husbandrie* was a perennial bestseller. First published is 1557, it went through six editions during the last seven years of the author's life. Sadly, Tusser does not seem to have heeded his own advice on the virtues of good husbandry. He died in a debtor's prison in 1580.

1574

The Hearbe of the Sunne

What did Europeans make of the sunflower? This and other new species were introduced to English readers in *Joyfull Newes out of the Newe Founde Worlde*, which was translated from a Spanish description of the Americas. "The hearbe of the Sunne," according to Nicolás Monardes, "is greater than a greate Platter or Dishe." To which he adds, with foresight, "It showeth marveilous faire in Gardines."

1577

Protecting Seedlings— Elizabethan-Style

Elizabethan gardeners went to great lengths to protect their seedlings from the dangers of frost. In *The Gardener's Labyrinth*, Thomas Hill describes a labor-intensive method that sounds more like house construction than horticulture. He instructs readers to first make "thick mattrasses of straw," then drive forked sticks into the corners and along the sides of the garden bed. Across these stick supports, place long wooden rods. Finally, rest the straw on the framework. "The mattrasses (when the sunne shineth warme) may be taken of, for the speedier increasing of the plantes springing up."

Tomatoes Are Bad for You

The English did not take to the American tomato. Foreigners—particularly the Spanish and Italians—might have actually eaten these *pomi d'oro* (golden apples) or "love apples," as they were sometimes called, but not the English. In the opinion of herbalist John Gerard, they were not only "of ranke and stinking savour," but were actually poisonous. This prejudice continued for more than two centuries, depriving the English settlers in North America of one of the most prolific and nutritious of garden plants.

1597

"Carrets" Are Good

Nowhere has the humble carrot received such lavish praise as in Richard Gardiner's *Profitable Instructions for the Manuring, Sowing and Planting of Kitchin Gardens.* "Sowe Carrets in your Gardens, and humbly praise God for them," he wrote. Keep a store of carrots, he urged. Then, if your city is besieged by the enemy, there will be an ample supply of nutritious food. Apart from carrots, Gardiner discussed cabbages, parsnips, turnips, lettuces, beans, onions, cucumbers, artichokes, and leeks. (Although the potato had arrived in Europe some 50 years earlier, Gardiner does not mention it.)

Gardiner wrote contemptuously of people who sold "olde or dead seedes." They were traitors and should be executed, he roared. He himself was a seed seller, and his book includes a list of prices: turnip seeds were 12 pence a pound; beans, 2 pence a quart.

1603

105

Nature in Harness

Gardening took on airs during the seventeenth century. The privileged classes of Europe and Asia created some of the most exquisite and ambitious landscapes ever conceived. A grand garden symbolized its master's power, offering "proof" that people had dominion over nature. Water splashed subserviently through channels and fountains. Flowers from all corners of the earth testified to their master's wealth. Shrubs assumed bizarre shapes under controlling shears. Extravagant sovereigns hired design geniuses to oversee the manicured symmetry of Versailles and the sublime vistas of the Taj Mahal.

Meanwhile, far from the cultivated estates of England and France, another breed of gardener was digging the earth. On the coast of the New World, settlers were gardening for their lives. Here was a winter cold that could destroy their crops overnight, a sun that scorched their seedlings as it never had in Northern Europe. The colonists viewed the natives—the only people who could help the newcomers in their struggle—with awe and contempt. Generations would pass before the colonists learned from America's indigenous people that humans and soil must serve and nourish each other. Driven by a sense of destiny and a desperate will to survive, Europeans in America gardened with the same passion to control nature as did the Old World aristocrats whom they had fled.

1609

Galileo Galilei builds a refracting telescope and begins using it to study the cosmos.

1617

William Lawson writes the first English gardening book targeted specifically at women; his *Country Housewife's Garden* is an instant hit.

1624

Architect, sculptor, and painter Gian Bernini begins working on St. Peter's in Rome.

1631

Ji Cheng writes a landcaping guide, urging readers to be creative—and safety-minded.

Hollyhocks are popular in England and New England; they're said to repel insects and cure skin ailments.

1606

William Shakespeare writes *King Lear*.

1621

Plimoth Plantation settlers write of fertilizing the corn fields with shad and alewife carcasses.

1615

Salomon de Caus builds a solar-powered motor.

1630

William Blackstone flees Puritans for Rhode Island and develops the first American apple cultivar, the 'Yellow Sweeting'.

1634

The Dutch fall in love with tulips; one small bulb is traded for 1,000 pounds of cheese, and then some.

1635

Spaniard Diego Rodriguez de Sílva y Velásquez paints *The Surrender of Breda.*

1661

Louis XIV builds Versailles, which contains formal gardens, lush hedges, sculpture, and fountains—as well as the Sun King's ego.

1638

Honeybees are introduced into the American colonies and soon escape from their hives, establish wild colonies, and supplant native species. Indians call them "the white man's fly."

1642

Blaise Pascal invents a calculating machine.

1667

John Milton's epic *Paradise Lost* is published; author sells copyright for £50.

1648

In Massachusetts, herbal healers are persecuted and tried for witchcraft.

1653

The Taj Mahal is built, containing shade-filled gardens and Mumtaz Mahal's tomb.

1665

The Great Plague strikes London.

1675

Mary Rowlandson describes the mostly foraged American Indian diet of "hartychoakes" and weeds.

1684

Isaac Newton theorizes about the force of gravity.

1690

European "weeding women" yank nettles to eke out a living.

1699

John Evelyn writes a guide to salads and extols the virtues of humble greens.

1701

Jethro Tull invents a machine seed drill.

1683

Dutch naturalist Antoni van Leeuwenhoek discovers bacteria.

1693

Versailles's gardener writes a tome about Louis XIV's kitchen garden, showing that seventeenth-century harvests were fit for a king.

1694

Rudolf Jakob Camerarius discovers plant pollen and demonstrates the sexuality of plants.

1682

The Carolinas' promoters lure Brits with promise of peaches and bountiful harvests.

1732

The threshing machine is invented by Michael Menzies.

1721

Johann Sebastian Bach composes his *Brandenburg Concertos.*

1727

The Irish oat crop fails, and potatoes run out; Jonathan Swift portrays poverty in Ireland.

1733

Jethro Tull scorns manure and suggests that his fellow Englishmen take up weeding.

1722

London smog, growing thicker with increasing industrialization, begins to choke vegetable gardens.

1726

The word "petals" is coined.

1731

Philip Miller writes his *Gardeners Dictionary,* recommending compost.

1737

Chinese Emperor Ch'ien-lung's walled paradise, the Garden of Perfect Brightness, features manmade mountains and rivers.

The Housewife Comes of Age

It was no secret that for centuries women had been doing much of the work in the household garden, but the first book in English to address a female audience specifically was *The Country Housewife's Garden* by William Lawson. This proved to be a shrewd publishing move, as the book quickly went through several editions. Lawson included practical ideas for kitchen and flower gardens, as well as designs for decorative knot gardens in which neatly trimmed shrubs—including rosemary, privet, thorn, roses, or sage—created a complex pattern, or knot, within a square plot.

1617

1621

"Manure" from the Sea

"We set the last spring some twenty acres of Indian corn, and sowed some six acres of barley and pease," wrote Edward Winslow from Plimoth Plantation to a friend in England, "and according to the manner of the Indians, we manured our ground with herring, or rather shads, which we have in great abundance." The corn did well, Winslow reported, but the peas were sown too late and withered in the North American sun.

Fish were an abundant source of fertilizer for the gardens of coastal New England. Every spring the alewives—members of the herring family—swarmed up the rivers from the sea, practically flinging themselves onto the fields. Ploughed in at 1,000 fish per acre, they significantly increased yields. "An acre thus dressed will produce and yield so much corn as three acres without fish," wrote colonist Thomas Morton in 1632. For the first two weeks after manuring with fish, farmers had to guard their aromatic fields against scavenging wolves and dogs. In some communities, the family pet hobbled pathetically around the gardens with one front paw tied to his neck to prevent him from digging up a snack of the rotting alewives.

Apples in the New World

The Puritans who sailed into Boston Harbor in 1630 were probably not expecting to find a solitary clergyman contentedly growing English apples and roses on Beacon Hill. William Blackstone was an ordained minister in the Church of England. He had come to Boston seven years earlier and stayed behind when his shipmates had returned home. Blackstone invited the new colonists to his side of the Charles River, where the water was purer, but relations between the Puritans and their host soured, and Blackstone—like so many religious dissidents after him—sought exile in Rhode Island. There his apple trees flourished, eventually producing America's first cultivar, the 'Yellow Sweeting'. Rhode Island's governor, Stephen Hopkins, proclaimed it "perhaps the richest and most delicious apple of the whole kind" in 1765.

| 1630

1631 |

The Versatile Hollyhock

John Winthrop, governor of the Massachusetts Bay Colony, was quick to order hollyhocks for his Boston garden. In 1631—a year after the Puritans settled in New England—John Winthrop Jr. purchased half an ounce of hollyhock seeds in London at his father's request. These were probably not intended to decorate the governor's flower garden; hollyhock leaves, when strewn on the floor, were used to repel insects. And as a medicine, hollyhocks were thought to heal wounds and lessen the itch of chilblains. Perhaps, though, Governor Winthrop was simply nostalgic for a taste of the Old World. Hollyhocks had been a familiar English "pot herbe" since the Roman conquest.

The Mountain Builder of Zhenjiang

When Ji Cheng, a middle-aged artist, settled in the eastern Chinese city of Zhenjiang, he scoffed at his neighbors' clumsy attempts at garden design. "Could you do any better yourself?" they challenged. He soon proved that he could. Ji Cheng's harmonious landscapes of water, rocks, and trees followed the great tradition of Chinese landscape gardening. Unlike any of his predecessors, however, Ji Cheng put his knowledge

1631

down in writing. His *Yüan Ye* (*The Craft of Gardens*) describes how to lay ornamental walkways, design pavilions, select rocks, and construct fantastic "mountains" that capture the spirit of wilderness within the walls of a garden. Urging his readers to create with emotion and imagination, Ji Cheng did not neglect the practical aspects of his craft. "If mountains are constructed among the women's apartments," he warned, "they should be solidly built as a precaution in case children play on them."

1634

Tulipomania

Europe fell in love with the tulip, but only the Dutch carried their passion to a calamitous extreme. Before 1575, very few Europeans had even heard of this brilliant newcomer from Turkey. By early in the seventeenth century, though, the tulip was a prized exhibit in the gardens of the wealthy. Especially valued in the Netherlands were the striped or flame-patterned varieties. Their prices were exorbitant. One sought-after bulb sold for 1,200 florins in 1624—the equivalent of at least as many dollars. Not surprisingly, less-privileged gardeners began to take notice. After all, they discovered, the tulip was not hard to cultivate. Tulip bulbs were soon changing hands at an uncontrollable rate and at ever-inflating prices. Then they stopped changing hands entirely. A consignment

The Dangers of "Practicing Physic"

Herbalism was an occasionally deadly practice in seventeenth-century New England. Although healers had been preparing medicines from plants since prehistory, attitudes were changing. The Church was determined to root out people who were "conversing with the devil" and was quick to detect satanic practices when patients sickened under the care of an herbal healer. Also, a newly emerging—and all-male—medical profession jealously looked for opportunities to discredit traditional healers, who were usually poor and female.

Even the most ordinary medicines could get an unlucky woman into trouble. Simply "practicing physic" was one of the charges that sent Margaret Jones of Charlestown, Massachusetts, to the gallows in 1648; her medicines were purported to be "such things as (by her confession) were harmless, as aniseed, liquors, etc., yet they had extraordinary violent effects." Testifying against Ann Burt of Lynn, Massachusetts, in 1670, Jacob Knight complained that "widow Burt" had given him a drink to cure a headache. His gripe: "When I had drunk of it, I was worse in my head." A local physician accused the same Ann Burt of causing a disease with "noe natural caus." Burt survived the assault, as did her granddaughter Elizabeth Proctor of Salem, Massachusetts. Proctor was said to have killed her neighbors by witchcraft for not taking her medicines. The accused woman, who was pregnant at the time of her trial, was freed when the witch-hunt hysteria subsided in 1693. Her husband, John, and nineteen others were among Salem's unfortunate victims of persecution.

of bulbs—while still in the ground—would be sold merely as investments to a second, third, and fourth party, none of whom had any interest in planting them. Between 1634 and 1637 "tulipomania" swept through the Netherlands. Desperate traders, down to their last guilder, bartered their belongings for a single bulb. One extravagant transaction involved loads of wheat and rye; eight pigs and 12 sheep; barrels of wine, beer, and butter; "1000 lbs. of cheese; a complete bed; a suit of clothes and a silver beaker"—all for a single specimen of the tulip bulb 'Victory'. The bubble burst, as many had predicted it would, leaving thousands penniless, possessionless, and embarrassed. But the Dutch never forsook the flower with which they'd enjoyed such a wild fling.

1653

Paradise in India

"Enter thou My Paradise," reads the inscription on the gateway to the Taj Mahal, in Agra. Many twenty-first-century visitors would agree that Shah Jahan's tomb for his wife, Mumtaz Mahal, brings paradise to mind. Shah Jahan, however, intended these words from the Koran to be taken literally. His devotion to his Persian wife was such that on her death in 1631 (during the birth of their 15th child) he was determined to lay her remains in a garden that came as close to the Islamic paradise as was humanly possible.

Like many Islamic gardens, those of the Taj Mahal include four water channels, symbolizing the four rivers of paradise. Less typically, Shah Jahan's architect placed the luminescent marble sepulchre at one

1661

Empire of the Sun King

Louis XIV, king of France from 1661 to 1715, set about creating the gardens at Versailles, southwest of Paris, as soon as he assumed the throne. He was a man without a shred of modesty—the Sun King, as he called himself—and his gardens reflected his enormous *amour propre* (or ego, as the English more plainly put it). Designed by a brilliant gardener named André Le Nôtre, Versailles was supposed to amaze its visitors. Fountains and sculpture, gracious promenades, radiating paths, labyrinthine hedges, a chessboard of formal gardens, and a mile-long canal—complete with its own navy—dazzled the king's guests. Everywhere there was symmetry; everywhere nature was controlled. Even the sun, Louis's personal motif, obediently followed his garden's east-west axis on August 25, the feast day of St. Louis. Versailles was a place of pleasure. Parties included jousting, opera, ballet, lavish pageants, and fireworks. The playwright Molière and the composer Lully were both on call for their king.

Louis did not separate business from pleasure, so in 1682 Versailles became the official seat of government. The garden, Europe's playground for years, became its political center as well—proof for any remaining skeptics that the earth was truly orbiting the sun.

end of the enclosure rather than in the middle. In the center is a raised marble pool, symbolizing the celestial tank of abundance where, it is said, Muhammad admits the faithful to paradise. The meaning of this symbolism may be lost on most of Agra's visitors, but the long vista created by the off-center tomb is nevertheless one of the most admired landscapes in the world. Missing from today's Taj Mahal are the lush plantings that originally gave the 20-acre garden a dark, exotic atmosphere. A French visitor in 1663 spoke of "garden paths shaded with trees, and many parterres full of flower." Sunbaked open spaces seem to have had no place in paradise.

Wild Harvest

In February 1675, Mary Rowlandson, a minister's wife in the tiny village of Lancaster, Massachusetts, was kidnapped by American Indians and held as a captive in the forest for nearly three months. "Their diet and commonest food was ground-nuts," she wrote of her captors. "They eat also nuts, and acorns, harty-choakes, lilly-roots, ground-beans, and several other weeds and roots that I know not." In fact, Indians of the eastern United States harvested more than 175 wild plants, while cultivating only a handful. Beans, corn, squash, sunflowers, and Jerusalem artichokes were their main garden crops. The forest provided all the other courses on the American Indian menu, from salads to fruits and nuts.

| 1682

Travel Brochures, Colonial-Style

In their efforts to entice new settlers to America, promoters published accounts of their colony's natural riches. "They have two crops of Indian corn in one year," boasted a pamphlet about the English settlement at Cape Fear. "Fruit trees there are in abundance of various and excellent kinds," claimed a South Carolina account. "The peach tree in incredible numbers grows wild." In the damp chill of Britain, many readers must have started packing their trunks.

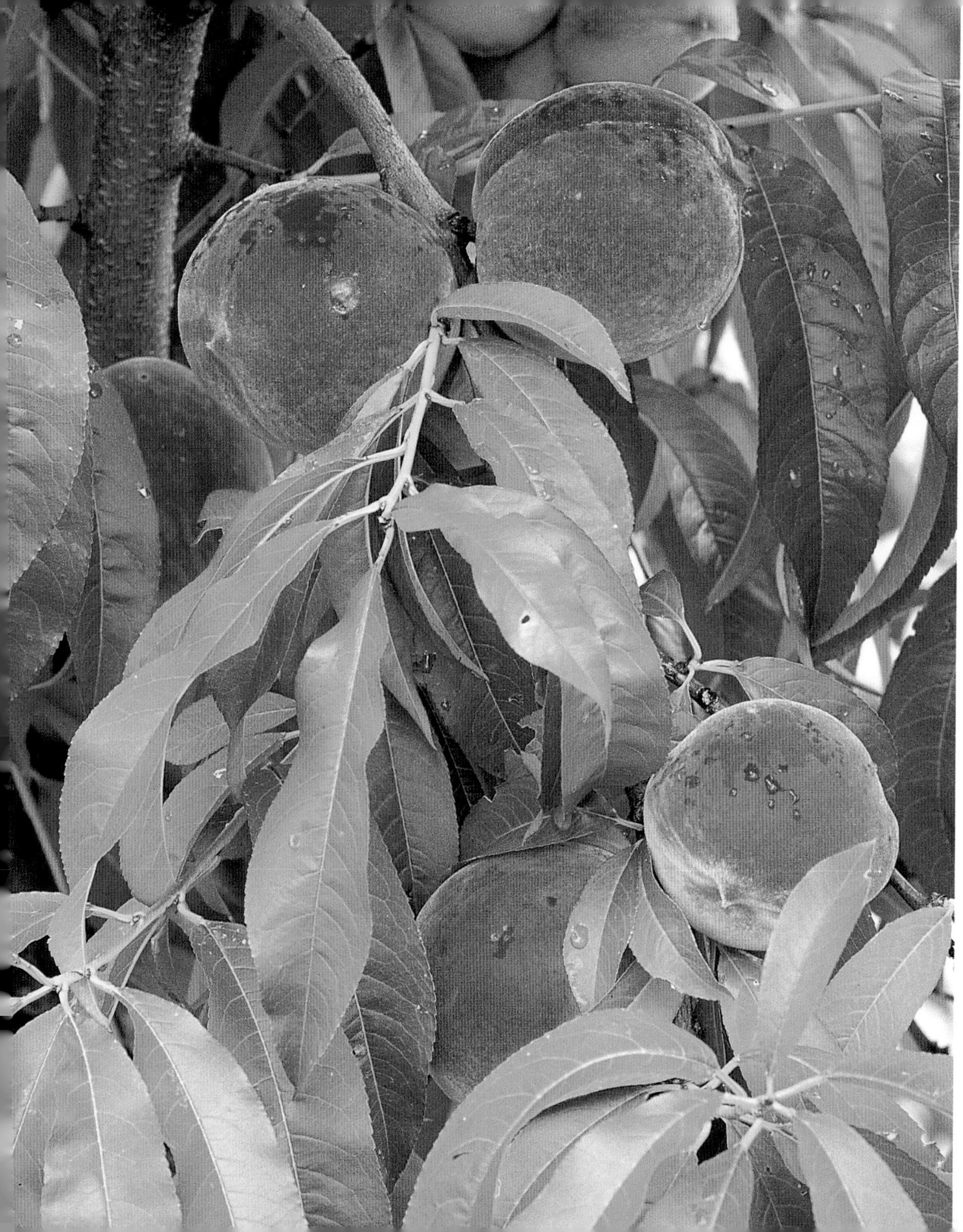

nature
in
harness

Weeding Women

Who did the dirty work in the grand gardens of Europe? At the very bottom of the huge labor pyramid were the "weeding women," employed to uproot nettles, drive away birds, sweep leaves, and squash pests. Their pay averaged less than half the amount of men's pay. At Hampton Court in 1696, male casual laborers received around 1½ shillings (18 pence) per day; women received 8 pence. The well-born Celia Fiennes, on a riding tour of England in 1690, remarked on a lifelike statue in the Duke of Bedford's cherry orchard, "a figure of stone resembling an old weeder woman," she wrote. The duke presumably thought the effigy was quaint, or perhaps it served as a scarecrow. A real live "old weeder woman" would doubtless have been grateful for a fraction of the fee paid to the sculptor.

125

Feeding the King

The word Versailles summons up images of fountains, sculptures, reflecting pools, and elegant promenades. But Versailles was not just a palace—it was the place that King Louis XIV and his enormous household called home. And like all seventeenth-century homes, Versailles had a kitchen garden: 25 acres of fruits and vegetables stocked the royal larders. This small farm was presided over by Jean de La Quintinye, who wrote a comprehensive textbook on the subject. *The Compleat Gard'ner*, as it was called in English, was intended for the landowner with a bank account (and pretensions) approaching that of the French king. To the modern reader, it offers a glimpse of the astonishing range of fruits and vegetables available in the seventeenth century. In one design for an orchard, Quintinye calls for 205 peach trees, including 23 different varieties. Pears are even more prolific. The author lists 50 "good pears," 44 "indifferent pears," 66 "bad pears," and 19 varieties of pears that, he judges, "I know to be so bad, that I counsel no body to plant any of them."

Anyone for Sow Thistle?

In an age when the roast beef of Olde England sat squarely on its throne, not many people spoke out in favor of salads. For this reason, the voice of diarist John Evelyn (1620–1706)—with all his antique syntax—seems positively modern. "I would recall the world," wrote Evelyn, "if not altogether to their pristine diet, yet to a much more wholesome and temperate than is now in fashion." Evelyn wrote more on this subject in *Acetaria: A Discourse of Sallets*. Evelyn's 73 "sallet" ingredients are enough to put a modern salad bar to shame. His list includes a number of unfamiliar and unappetizing ingredients—viper grass, sow thistle, and blite, among them—as well as the more reassuring cucumber, Spanish onion, and parsley. Then, as now, lettuce was the foundation for any good salad, though Evelyn gives it powers that seem almost supernatural. Among other qualities, lettuce "extinguishes thirst, excites appetite, kindly nourishes, and above all represses vapours, conciliates sleep, mitigates pain; besides the effect it has upon the morals, Temperance and Chastity." With lettuce like this, other ingredients seem superfluous.

Gardening in the City

Anyone trying to garden in London during the early eighteenth century had to contend with choking smog and cramped, ill-lit courtyards. These were the enthusiasts whom Thomas Fairchild addressed in *The City Gardener*. "I find that everything will not prosper in London," he observed, "either because the smoke of the sea-coal does hurt to some plants, or else because those people, who have little gardens in London, do not know how to manage their plants." A London gardener with 30 years of experience, Fairchild advised his readers on flower gardening in city squares, sodden riverside plots, balconies, window boxes, and tiny, dark backyards. His recommendations for hardy city plants included at least two newcomers from America: the sunflower and the scarlet runner bean.

1726

The Leaves of a Flower

What do you call those colorful, often showy things growing around the outside parts of a flower? It is hard to believe that the English language did not have a word for them until partway into the seventeenth century. In 1649 a Latin word was first proposed: *petalum*, which is derived from the Greek *petalon*, meaning leaf. In 1726 the word was at last defined simply but clearly: "Petals: Leaves of a flower; so-called to distinguish them from the green leaves of the plant."

127

128

Buttermilk and Potatoes

Jonathan Swift, author of *Gulliver's Travels,* took a grim survey of his native Ireland in 1727. The poor were "living in filth and nastiness upon buttermilk and potatoes," he bitterly observed, with "not a shoe or stocking to their feet, or a house so convenient as an English hog-sty to receive them." That year the oat crop failed, and the Irish were forced to fall back on potatoes entirely. Many died of starvation when the winter supplies of potatoes were exhausted.

How to Garden, from "Abies" to "Ziziphus"

No one who was serious about gardening in Britain or America was without a copy of Philip Miller's *Gardeners Dictionary.* "When one has it," commented an eighteenth-century Swedish scientist, "no other book is afterwards required." Thomas Jefferson owned a well-thumbed copy; so did Lord Chesterfield. Miller's *Dictionary* examined all known plants from "Abies: the Firr Tree" to "Ziziphus; the Jujube." As the director of London's internationally famous Chelsea Physic Garden, Miller was an expert on all aspects of his craft, from pruning to constructing garden paths. He included nine recipes for compost, some of them serving as mini-lessons in social history. For "a compost that will hasten the growth of plants," he suggested, "take four loads of stiff soil, two loads of malt grains after brewing, and four loads of sand."

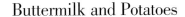

THE GARDENERS DICTIONARY:
CONTAINING
The Best and Newest METHODS
OF
CULTIVATING and IMPROVING
THE
Kitchen, Fruit, Flower Garden, and Nursery;
As also for Performing the
Practical Parts of AGRICULTURE:
INCLUDING
The MANAGEMENT of VINEYARDS,
WITH THE
Methods of MAKING and PRESERVING WINE,
According to the present Practice of
The most skilful Vignerons in the several Wine Countries in *Europe.*
TOGETHER WITH
DIRECTIONS for PROPAGATING and IMPROVING,
From real Practice and Experience,
ALL SORTS OF TIMBER TREES.
THE EIGHTH EDITION,
Revised and Altered according to the latest SYSTEM of BOTANY; and
Embellished with several COPPER-PLATES, which were not in some former Editions.
By PHILIP MILLER, F.R.S.
Gardener to the Worshipful Company of Apothecaries, at their Botanic Garden
in *Chelsea,* and Member of the Botanic Academy at *Florence.*
... *Digna manes divini gloria ruris.* VIRG. Georg.
LONDON,
Printed for the AUTHOR;
And Sold by JOHN and FRANCIS RIVINGTON, at No. 62, St. *Paul's Church-yard*; A. MILLAR,
J. WHISTON, W. STRAHAN, W. JOHNSTON, B. BALDWIN, B. WHITE, T. LONGMAN,
W. CLARKE and R. COLLINS, W. JOHNSTON, T. CASLON, T. CADELL, T. LOWNDS,
B. LAW, C. RIVINGTON, J. DODSLEY, T. DAVIES, T. PAYNE.
S. BLADON, G. ROBINSON and J. ROBERTS.
M.DCC.LXVIII.

1731

A Man of the Soil

Jethro Tull (1674–1741) refused to believe that plants took their principal nutrients from water, fire, or air—a notion held by many of his fellow Englishmen. In his classic text, *Essay on the Principles of Tillage and Vegetation* (1733), Tull argued that soil was the chief source of plant nutrition. Keep the earth nourished, weed-free, and well cultivated, he maintained, and your crops would thrive. In one simple experiment he demonstrated that weeds would stunt the growth of wheat, not by crowding out the grain, as was generally held, but by depriving the soil of nutrients. Tull was not so enlightened when it came to manure, which he considered to be of little importance. Dung encouraged pests and gave vegetables a bad flavor, he claimed.

1733

The Garden of Perfect Brightness

The French Jesuits who lived at the court of Emperor Ch'ien-lung in Peking were not easily amazed by grand gardens. The Renaissance back home, after all, had produced marvels of opulent landscape designs. Northwest of the Imperial City, however, was a garden that took their breath away. Yuan Ming Yuan, the Garden of Perfect Brightness, or the Garden of Gardens, was the Chinese Versailles, but it was similar to the French king's garden only in its grandeur. Its 60,000 acres, enclosed by a wall, were carefully fashioned to capture the wild spirit of nature. Manmade mountains rose above lakes and rivers, and each bay or channel had been artfully planned. "The banks are sprinkled with flowers," wrote Father Attiret, "as if they had been produced there naturally." Unlike Versailles, little at Yuan Ming Yuan survives today. In 1860, British soldiers looted and destroyed the gardens, setting fire to nearly 2,000 ornamental buildings.

1737

From Frontier to Front Lawns

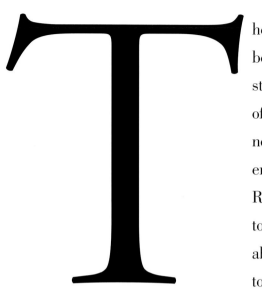

The eighteenth century wore on and a funny thing began happening to Europe's formal gardens. The straight lines and square plots dissolved in favor of more "natural" landscapes. In fact, these were not natural at all, but the work of skilled designers who discarded the rigid symmetry of the Renaissance, arranging trees, rocks, and flowers to simulate nature. There was nothing natural about the process. Cottage gardens were torn up to make room for uninterrupted vistas. Kitchen gardens, too unsightly, were neatly tucked away behind walls.

This new philosophy did not affect many gardeners in the North American colonies, soon to be the United States. On the western frontier, the natural look was for real. The kitchen garden was the heart of the household, the place that would determine a family's survival. Further east, a century and a half of European settlement had created grand estates and thriving gardens. For many Americans, however, gardening was primarily a matter of producing food. To George Washington and Thomas Jefferson, a leader's responsibilities were as much horticultural as political.

And on both sides of the Atlantic, a middle class blossomed—city dwellers who loved to garden but who had little time or space to play with. The future of gardening, as we define it today, was in their hands.

1739

Royal botanist John Bartram catalogs and crossbreeds flowers in Pennsylvania, creating striking results.

1744

Frederick II distributes free seed potatoes to reluctant Prussian peasants and makes them an offer they can't refuse: Soldiers enforce his edict that the peasants plant potatoes or risk having their ears and noses cut off.

1753

Carolus Linnaeus's *Species plantarum* is published.

1769

Nicolas-Joseph Cugnot invents a steam-powered tractor.

1760

President Washington delights in soil experiments.

1743

The American Philosophical Society is founded and examines gardening as patriotic duty.

1752

Chinese roses first arrive in Europe.

1759

England's Augusta sets aside acreage on her estate to found Kew Gardens, which will grow to have an impressive plant collection.

SHAKERS' STRING BEANS.

1774

People in the Prussian town of Kolberg would rather starve than eat potatoes.

1785

Oliver Evans invents the automatic gristmill.

1790

New York State Shakers sell seeds in convenient, small envelopes.

1792

The *Farmer's Almanack* is first published by Robert B. Thomas.

1796

Aloys Senefelder invents lithography.

1783

Garden designer Capability Brown dies, leaving behind a legacy of fierce control of nature.

1787

Garden calendars are published in Charleston, South Carolina.

1791

Wolfgang Amadeus Mozart composes his *Requiem*.

1793

Eli Whitney fashions the cotton gin.

1778

Joseph Bramah invents the flush toilet.

1798

Empress Josephine gardens and studies botany at Malmaison; and she will commission the artist Pierre-Joseph Redouté to depict her flowers.

1800

The Library of Congress is established in Washington, D.C.

1803

Thomas Jefferson gardens zealously.

1819

William Cobbett critiques the wild American spirit of gardening.

The Language of Flowers, by Charlotte de Latour, confounds lovers.

John Keats writes "Ode to a Nightingale."

1812

Sculptor Antonio Canova completes his *Venus Italica*.

1802

Alexander von Humboldt discovers mountains of guano off Peru and realizes that nitrate-rich droppings are useful as fertilizer.

1810

Peter Gaillard invents a mowing machine.

1817

Hybrid roses steal the scene in Europe and the United States.

1821

John Constable paints *The Hay Wain*.

1822

Johnny Appleseed plants orchards and earns his nickname.

1831

Cyrus McCormick invents a reaping machine.

1835

John Loudon writes *Encyclopedia of Gardening*, explaining garden design and large-pest control.

1820

Colonel Robert Gibbon Johnson disproves the myth that eating nightshades will kill you; he eats a tomato on the Salem County, New Jersey, courthouse steps and fails to drop dead immediately.

1824

Ludwig van Beethoven completes his Ninth Symphony.

1830

Edwin Budding invents the lawn mower.

1837

The first steel plowshare is developed by American blacksmith John Deere.

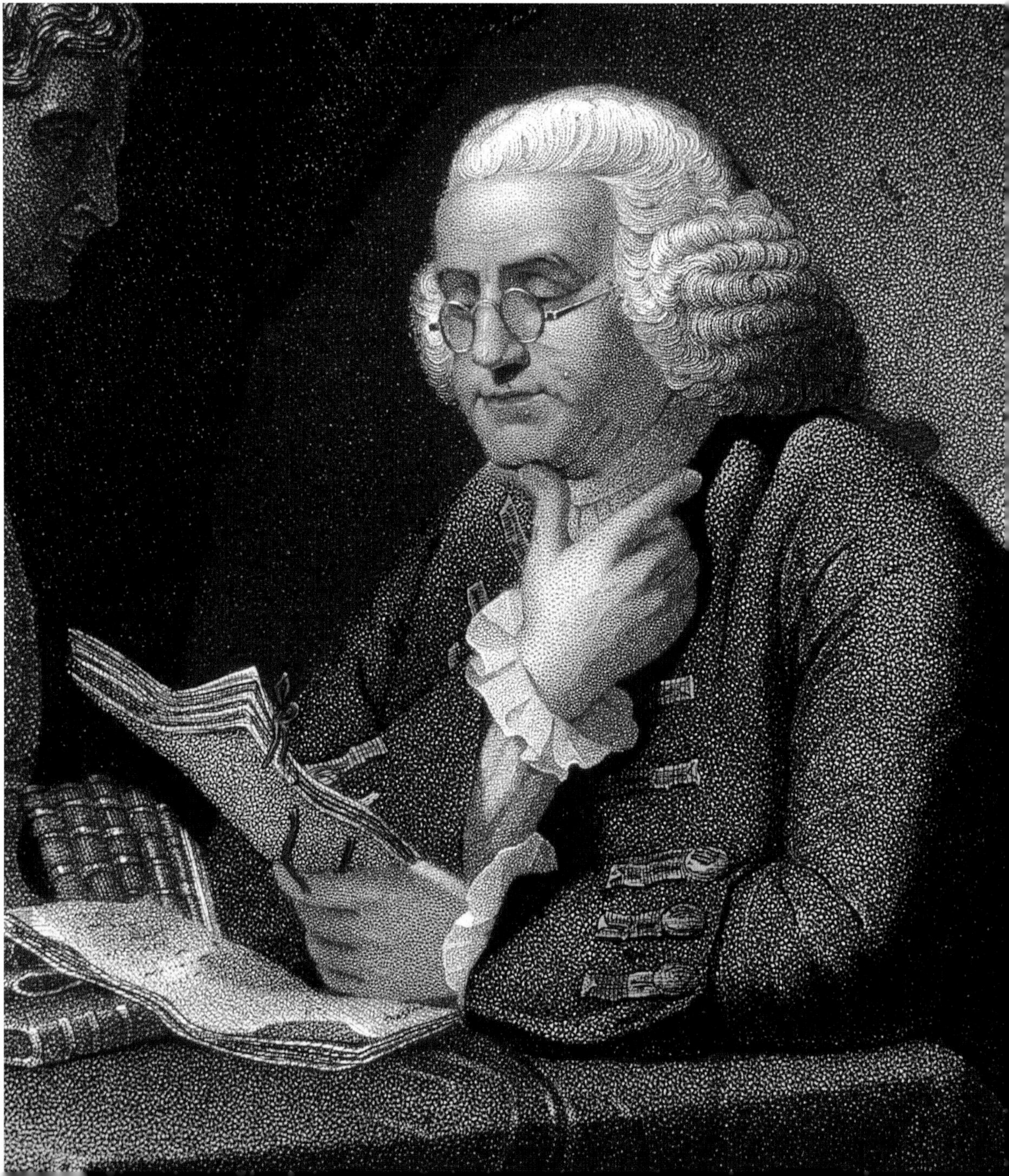

1739

Curiously Colorful Flowers

Europe learned about the plants of North America from a modest Pennsylvanian Quaker named John Bartram (1699–1777). Appointed as the official American botanist by King George III, Bartram sent back hundreds of new specimens—from the sugar maple to skunk cabbage—to his colleagues in the Old World. In 1739 he experimented with cross-breeding, through which he "obtained curious mixed colors in flowers, never known before." According to Swedish botanist Carolus Linnaeus, Bartram was "the greatest natural botanist in the world." His son William carried on John's botanical expeditions and is considered the first—and still among the finest—of nature writers from the New World.

1743

Serve Your Country: Discover a Plant

"The first drudgery of settling new colonies is now pretty well over," wrote Benjamin Franklin (pictured at left) in 1743. The time had come, he declared, "to improve the common stock of knowledge." So was born the American Philosophical Society. Among the many areas that members of the society investigated, gardening was central. In the words of Thomas Jefferson—president of the Society in 1796, president of the United States in 1801—"The greatest service which can be rendered any country is to add a useful plant to its culture."

Rosa Est Rosa Est Rosa

Before Carolus Linnaeus, a rose was not always a rose. While attempts had been made to establish a universal scientific classification of plants and animals, no one with sufficient knowledge and persistence had devoted a lifetime to the task. Linnaeus was just such a systematic genius. Born Carl von Linné in 1707 to a poor family in Sweden, he revealed an early passion for natural sciences, and before he was 30, he had established an international reputation in botany. His major achievement was developing a binomial, or two-name, system for classifying plants and animals, replacing the wordy and inconsistent system that had previously confused Europe's scientists. Thus, according to Linnaeus's *Species plantarum* (published in 1753), a rose would always be classified as the genus *Rosa* followed by a single Latin adjective describing the precise species: *Rosa canina* (dog rose) or *Rosa chinensis* (China rose). Although there have been many subsequent modifications made to the Linnaean system, the essence of his scheme has remained intact.

Kew Gardens

A passion for plants from all parts of the world seized the rulers of Europe in the eighteenth century. One of the most famous collections was established at Kew, the London arboretum on the River Thames. Here, the princess Augusta, mother of George III, devoted part of her estate to exotic species from Britain's expanding empire. Scientists from the Royal Botanic Gardens accompanied every major scientific expedition or diplomatic mission, returning with shiploads of plants—some taken by guile or even force—to be housed in Kew's elegant greenhouses. Known today simply as Kew Gardens, Augusta's few acres grew to become a botanical symbol of Britain's imperial might.

1760

First Gardener

The "Father of His Country" was also one of its most distinguished farmers. In 1760, George Washington recorded an experiment he conducted with ten different soil types, including mixtures of earth, sand, clay, and various manures. "Mixed my composts in a box with ten compartments," he noted. "Planted each with three grains of wheat, oats and barley in rows, equal depths, done by a machine." Washington took more than a scientific interest in gardening. "I am led to reflect," he wrote to an English agriculturalist, "how much more delightful to an undebauched mind is the task of making improvements on the earth, than all the vain glory which can be acquired from ravaging it."

1774

Just Say "No" to Potatoes

It was a widespread belief in eighteenth-century Europe that the physical appearance of a vegetable determined its qualities and influenced the health of the person who consumed it. The typical potato of the day—much lumpier than modern varieties—was clearly bad for the skin. Surely it caused leprosy, or that ulcerous skin condition known as scrofula. So great was the resistance to the potato that many people just said "no," even if the alternative was starvation. When Frederick the Great of Prussia sent a shipment of potatoes to relieve a famine in  Kolberg in 1774, the reply was uncompromising: "The things have neither smell nor taste, not even the dogs will eat them, so what are they to us?"

1783

The Reign of Capability Brown

When landscape designer Lancelot "Capability" Brown died in 1783, King George III remarked to his gardener, "Now, Mellicent, you and I can do here what we please." The king was scarcely exaggerating. Capability Brown's designs for great gardens and parks held absolute dominion over the aristocratic estates of eighteenth-century England. His landscapes of meadows, irregularly shaped lakes, and artfully scattered trees softened the rigid geometric plantings of the Renaissance, emphasizing the natural aspects of a landscape. Like all revolutions, this one came at a cost. Formal avenues of trees were leveled and cottage gardens were obliterated in the passion for Brown's new natural look.

1787

Gardening in Charleston

The fortunate gardeners of Charleston, South Carolina, could turn to a number of regional publications for practical assistance. Robert Squibb, a seed importer familiar with all the latest varieties and techniques, instructed his readers in "the modern art of gardening," taking them month by month through the year's tasks in his *Gardener's Calendar*. Another, much shorter *Gardeners Kalender* was the work of Martha Daniel Logan, daughter of the governor and long-time resident of Charleston. These two *Calendars* serve to contrast the old and the new in gardening practices. In April, for instance, both writers call for planting carrots and parsnips, but only Logan insists, "let it be on the full of the moon." Squibb could not have objected to Logan's pungent recipe for "a liquor to steep Windsor beans": "Take three quarts of sheep dung, two quarts of pigeons, four quarts of fowls, and six quarts of well rotted horse dung…pour eight gallons of water on it, stirring it well and frequently."

Squibb's modernity went only so far. A sobering appendix at the end of his *Calendar* reminds the reader just who was doing most of the dirty work: "Ladies or Gentlemen who would wish to have three or four Negro Boys (from fourteen to sixteen years of age) instructed in the modern art of Gardening, may apply as above."

Seed Envelopes on the Scene

An English visitor to New York State in the 1850s was surprised that the best source of seeds and plants was the Shaker community in New Lebanon. Like many Englishmen, he had heard only joking references to this austere and eccentric sect. In fact, the Shakers had been selling seeds since the 1790s. Starting with a few boxes of vegetable seeds, the Shakers began to make a name—and a profit— for themselves in the seed trade. For such devout, unworldly people, they showed surprising business acumen. Shakers were the first to sell seeds in printed envelopes, and they advertised in eye-catching color. The quality of their product owed less to business management than to the Shakers' reverence for life. "If you love a plant, and take heed of what it likes," observed Elder Frederick Evans, "you will be repaid by it."

The Roses of Malmaison

Marie-Josèphe-Rose Tascher de La Pagerie is known to history as Josephine, the passionate and wildly extravagant wife of Napoléon Bonaparte. From 1798, she kept house at their chateau Malmaison. There she indulged in the fantasies of the very rich: rare black swans, a house decorated with the plunders of her husband's Italian campaign, and a private menagerie with an orangutan who wore a negligee and curtsied to visitors. But when it came to plants, Josephine revealed a serious side. "Her taste for botany was no mere caprice, but the basis of study, and serious study at that," wrote an acquaintance. "She soon knew the names of all the plants, the family they were classified as belonging to by naturalists, their origins and their properties."

Josephine's ambition was to distribute collections of her rare plants to each *département* in France. Her principal contribution to gardening, however, was to commission Pierre-Joseph Redouté, an artist famous for his botanical accuracy and delicacy of design, to illustrate the flowers of Malmaison. From 1802 to 1816, Redouté produced 502 engraved plates of Malmaison lilies alone, but he is best known for the nearly 200 engravings of rose varieties Josephine planted in her garden. Josephine, who died in 1814, never saw a volume of Redouté's *Les Roses.* The artist himself died at the age of 80 while drawing a lily.

Guano for the Garden

The German scientist Alexander von Humboldt (1769–1859) was a leader in many areas of science. Geography, meteorology, botany, and oceanography were his specialties, but he also made a significant—though unglamorous—contribution to gardening. While exploring the coast of Peru, he discovered just how the Peruvian Indians had gardened for centuries. They fertilized their crops with guano, which had built up to 30 feet deep on some coastal islands. Europe was slow to respond to von Humboldt's enthusiasm. Not until 1840 did an English scientist make a powerful case for the discovery, showing that one ton of bird droppings has the same amount of nitrogen and phosphates as 33 tons of horse manure. The guano rush was on, with England importing nearly 300,000 tons of the miracle fertilizer in 1845.

A Gardener in the White House

"I thank you for the seeds and stones you have been so kind as to send me," wrote Thomas Jefferson to Governor John Milledge in November 1803. "I hope that Congress will rise early enough to let me pass the month of March at home to superintend the planting them." The President's mind was never far from his beloved gardens at Monticello. In 1809, after four years as U.S. vice president and eight as president, he retired with joy to his Virginia home to supervise the construction of his terraced kitchen garden: 1 acre of vegetables in a plot 1,000 feet long, and 7 acres of fruits, berries, and "Indian" plants, all fenced in against marauding deer and rabbits. That year he planted vegetables in 154 numbered beds.

Jefferson combined a scientist's curiosity with a gardener's passion. New seeds and cuttings were continually entering and leaving his house. In 1803 he was thrilled to authorize a long-cherished dream—the exploration of America's West under the leadership of his private secretary, Meriwether Lewis, and William Clark. Later he experimented with the salsify and snap beans that Lewis brought back for him. His passion for gardening did not fade with age. While suffering from his final illness, at the age of 83, he sent for seed from an improved variety of cucumber. During retirement he wrote, "Though an old man, I am but a young gardener."

The Revolutionary Rose

Which of these items is out of place: Robespierre, Simon Bolivar, George Washington, or 'Parson's Pink China'? The answer: none of the above. All were revolutionaries, and although one is a rose and not a man, its influence on history is nonetheless significant.

For centuries Europeans had lovingly cultivated "summer roses," varieties that flowered only once during the season. But rebellion—in the rose beds as on the streets—was in the air. Trade with the Far East introduced Europe and America to *Rosa chinensis,* the perpetually flowering roses of China. 'Parson's Pink China', one of the leaders of this invasion, hybridized naturally with a European rose, opening up a world of new blooms known as the Bourbon roses. Other hybrids, both accidental and designed, would contribute to the season-long displays of the modern rose garden.

Say It with Flowers

Flowers spoke a silent language in nineteenth-century Europe. When lovers wished to communicate secretly, they had a code at their disposal. First fully described by Charlotte de Latour in a book entitled *The Language of Flowers*, floral messages became the craze, first in France and then throughout the continent. In Latour's "language," each flower had a meaning. The carnation, for instance, signified "lively and pure love"; the acacia, "Platonic love." The arrangement of a bouquet—even the placement of a single flower—also spoke volumes. "Stripped of its thorns, the rose means 'there is everything to hope for,' " explained Latour. A bouquet of roses meant "see you at one o'clock." Change the flowers to heliotropes, however, and you were meeting at two. Latour's book spawned many imitators and intense analysis. Europe's florists were the most obvious beneficiaries.

151

1819

A Critical Look at American Gardens

According to Englishman William Cobbett, American gardens were not up to Old World standards. "America has soil and climate far surpassing those of England; and yet she is surprisingly deficient in variety as well as quality of garden products," observed this tireless social critic. Part of the problem, Cobbett believed, was that there was simply too much land in the New World. People would do better gardening intensively on a single acre than squandering the resources of one hundred. Another problem was the overconfident, can-do-it colonial mentality. "Every man, who can dig and hoe and rake, calls himself a gardener as soon as he lands here from England," he complained. Not lacking confidence himself, Cobbett set about instructing the Americans on how to garden. "The object evidently is to cause the art of gardening to be better understood," he wrote in *The American Gardener*. "There is, in this case, plenty of room for improvement."

John "Appleseed" Chapman

Even during his life, John Chapman accumulated tall tales. Legend says he dressed in rags, preached the gospel, and walked barefoot through winter. He shared sleeping quarters with bears, spared the lives of rattlesnakes, and put out his fires so mosquitoes would not die in the coals. He knew Washington and Lincoln. And—of course—he planted just about every apple orchard east of the Mississippi. As "John Appleseed" (a name first used in 1822), Chapman became an American icon.

There is more than a seed of truth in the legend of Johnny Appleseed. Chapman was born in Massachusetts in 1775. He was a nurseryman and made a scant living selling seedlings to settlers of Ohio and Indiana. On

his travels he evangelized for Emanuel Swedenborg's Church of the New Jerusalem, but he converted few. More successful were his orchards. According to the records of Dublin Township, Ohio, he leased a plot "for the purpose of sowing appleseeds on," promising to pay a rent of 1,000 apple trees over the next decade. Appleseed's legend lives on: No one can say exactly where Johhny Appleseed was buried, but several reliable witnesses have reported seeing his ghost.

1822

a   *b*   *c*   *d*

Farewell to the Scythe

When someone refers to a closely cut lawn as a "carpet," they are thinking like Edwin Budding, the under-rated English genius who invented the lawn mower. Inspired by the machinery that cuts the pile on textiles, Budding came up with the very recognizable ancestor of the modern push mower. In replacing the ancient scythe as the principal cutting instrument, Budding revolutionized grass care and in a single stroke made the suburban lawn possible. The lawn mower found powerful allies—Queen Victoria was quick to order a horse-drawn model. The commoner, however, had to manage without pony power. "It is particularly adapted for amateurs," wrote the influential garden writer Jane Loudon in 1844, "affording an excellent exercise to the arms and every part of the body."

Building a Better Mantrap

Are trespassers unearthing your carrots or making off with your prize peaches? John Loudon's *Encyclopedia of Gardening* gave the nineteenth-century solution. Under the heading "Machines for Destroying Vermin and for Defense against the Enemies of Gardens," Loudon (the husband of garden writer Jane Loudon) describes two "engine-traps for man." These are classified as "the common and the humane." The first "is a rat-trap on a large scale." Loudon admits that it is "a barbarous contrivance, though rendered absolutely necessary in the exposed gardens around great towns." The humane mantrap, on the other hand, "simply breaks the leg, and therefore is comparatively entitled to the appellation of humane."

There was much more to Loudon than mayhem. His two-volume *Encyclopedia* was by far the most popular and comprehensive such work available in English, covering all aspects of garden craft, science, history, and public policy. There has never been an encyclopedia since Loudon's to include a chemical analysis of cow urine, a discussion on gardening in Poland, advice on designing a labyrinth—and two methods of breaking a man's legs.

The Age of Enthusiasm

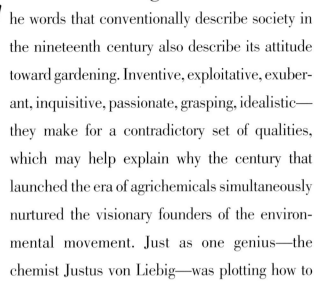

The words that conventionally describe society in the nineteenth century also describe its attitude toward gardening. Inventive, exploitative, exuberant, inquisitive, passionate, grasping, idealistic—they make for a contradictory set of qualities, which may help explain why the century that launched the era of agrichemicals simultaneously nurtured the visionary founders of the environmental movement. Just as one genius—the chemist Justus von Liebig—was plotting how to pump the soil full of chemicals, another genius—the naturalist Henry David Thoreau—was preaching the gospel of leaving the land alone.

Perhaps what most typifies the high Victorian era is the energy and passion with which its actors threw themselves into the business of life. In gardening, this zeal created seed dealers who would sell their souls for a milder radish or a straighter runner bean, scientists who convinced themselves that life on Earth depended upon their own particular fertilizer or pesticide, breeders who devoted their lives to creating a yellower rose, and landscape architects who equated garden design with morality.

Where were the ordinary men and women throughout all of this turmoil? They were where they have always been: in their gardens. They were trimming their hedges, thinning their carrots, battling aphids, and with increasing frequency, mowing their lawns.

1840

German chemist Justus von Liebig advocates measuring and controlling the soil's nutrients.

1842

The first chemical fertilizers are manufactured in London.

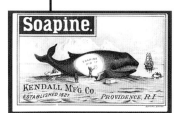

Gardeners use age-old and new-fangled pest controls, such as whale-oil soap.

1847

American gardener Robert Buist repeats old—but sound—advice: manure.

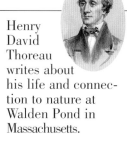

Henry David Thoreau writes about his life and connection to nature at Walden Pond in Massachusetts.

1851

Americans swallow tomato pills to cure cholera.

1841

Syracuse, New York, hosts the first state agricultural fair.

1846

Phytophthora infestans invades Ireland, potatoes die, and nearly a million Irish peasants starve.

1850

The American Vegetarian Society is founded. Its members see vegetarianism as the road to civil and spiritual reform.

1849

Crabgrass is patented.

1853

Seed catalogs hit mailboxes throughout the United States.

The 'Concord' grape is exhibited at the Massachusetts Horticultural Society and will soon spread across the country.

1856

U.S. president Pierce's Guano Islands Act claims all "unclaimed" islands in the name of the Stars and Stripes.

1863

Edouard Manet paints *Olympia*.

1865

Botanist Joseph Hooker takes charge of the evergrowing Kew Gardens.

The Thirteenth Amendment to the U.S. Constitution is passed, abolishing slavery.

1854

Showy Brits build the Crystal Palace, a symbol of national pride.

1860

British troops ravage the Chinese Garden of Perfect Brightness, burning and destroying gardens and buildings.

1866

Gregor Mendel studies peas, quietly breaking ground in genetics.

1867

Farmers use insecticides containing arsenic.

THE COLORADO BEETLE

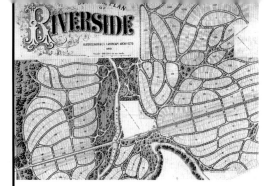

1868

Americans flock to Frederick Law Olmsted's carefully planned suburbs.

1882

W. Atlee Burpee holds gardening contests and offers new plant varieties through its ever-popular seed catalog.

1885

Belgian king Leopold II forms the Congo Free State.

Vincent Van Gogh paints *The Potato Eaters*.

1869

The Suez Canal is opened.

1882

Italy, Germany, and Austria-Hungary form a military pact, the Triple Alliance.

1874

DDT is invented by Othmar Zeidler.

1884

French botanist Pierre-Marie-Alexis Millardet concocts Bordeaux mixture, a solution of copper sulfate, water, and lime, to protect grapevines from fungal diseases.

1889

Philadelphia seed company Johnson and Stokes introduces the 'Brandywine' tomato.

1894

W. Atlee Burpee welcomes 'Iceberg' lettuce into the world. Its soul mate, Thousand Island dressing, is invented 20 years later in Clayton, New York.

1897

The hand-powered wheel hoe reaches its height in popularity.

The "Planet Jr." No. 1 Combined Drill and Wheel Hoe.

No. 1822I. This is the most popular combined tool known, and its friends have gained by substantial merit alone. It won the highest and only award at the cago Exposition. As a seed sower it is identical with the No. 2 "Planet Jr." II, except in size, and has all its merits, its strength, durability, ease of opera

1900

A French botanist crossbreeds roses to produce the everblooming 'Soleil d'Or'.

1909

The U.S. Bureau of Soils pronounces soil an "indestructable" resource.

1911

The pesticide BT is isolated and named, but it won't be sold in the United States for another half-century.

1895

Japan defeats China at war; China recognizes Korea's independence.

1902

The British defeat the Dutch in the South African Boer War.

Botanist Beatrix Potter's *The Tale of Peter Rabbit* is published.

1910

Marie Curie writes her *Treatise on Radioactivity.*

1899

English garden designer Gertrude Jekyll writes *Wood and Garden* and designs tranquil, preindustrial-style cottage gardens.

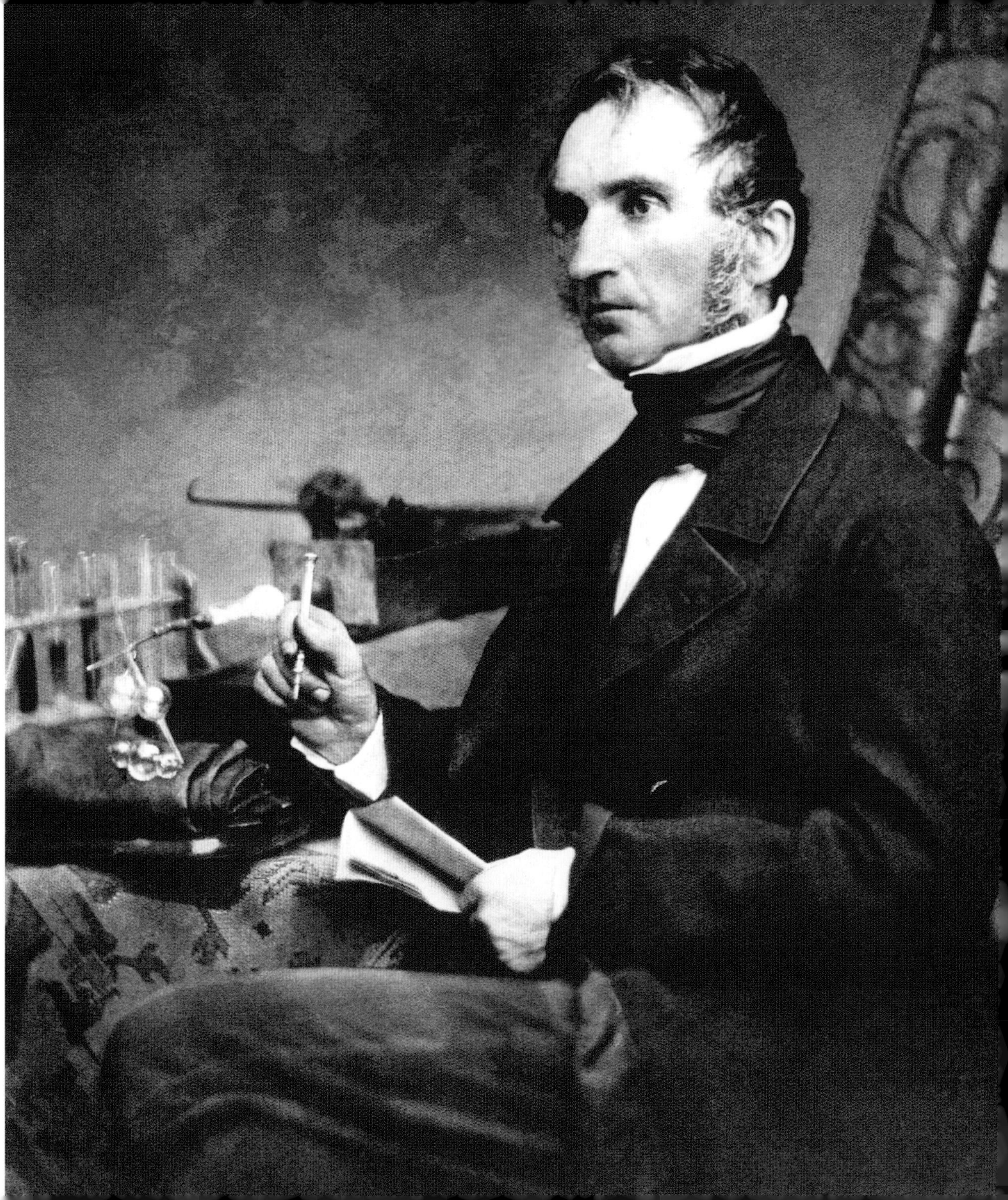

Science of the Soil

Why were the farms of the eastern United States not producing the same abundant crops that they had a century earlier? In their first enthusiasm for settling this vast, fertile land, America's new inhabitants had neglected some of the effective and time-honored procedures of traditional agriculture, leaving the soil depleted. Many people simply moved west. Those left behind sought a way to restore their worn-out soil.

One solution to this problem came from a surprising source. A young German scientist, formerly known for his work in organic chemistry, turned his attention to what makes plants grow. Justus von Liebig (1803–73) was no farmer, and he refused to honor the powerful, almost mystical belief that humus contained some vital life force essential to plants. Instead, he argued that plants absorbed dissolved nutrients from the soil. "The crops on a field," he wrote, "diminish or increase in exact proportion to the diminution or increase of the mineral substances conveyed to it in manure." In *Chemistry in Its Application to Agriculture and Physiology*, von Liebig established the importance of potassium, soda, lime, and magnesia to plants. Furthermore, he wrote that their effects could be measured. Why not produce them artificially and end this old-fashioned hit-or-miss agriculture? Liebig's propositions launched an era of experimentation with synthetic fertilizers. For better and for worse, the modern science of agriculture was born.

From Bonemeal to Agrichemicals

Bonemeal was in such demand as a fertilizer by British farmers that the domestic supply became inadequate. Looking abroad for a new source of this phosphorus-rich nutrient, Britannia was far from picky. "Already, in her eagerness for bones, she has turned up the battlefields of Leipzig, of Waterloo, and of the Crimea," complained the chemist Justus von Liebig. Responding to the fertilizer crisis, a young British agriculturist named John Bennet Lawes discovered that treating bones with sulfuric acid made the phosphorus more readily available. In 1842 he opened a factory in London for manufacturing chemical fertilizers. Manufacturers in Baltimore and Boston followed suit within a decade. The age of agrichemicals had begun.

First, Catch Your Whale

In the centuries before chemical agriculture, gardeners concocted their own insecticides from a range of relatively harmless ingredients. These might include soaps, sulfur, tobacco, lime, pepper, hellebore powder, vinegar, and the essences of various bitter herbs. In 1842, David Haggerston of Watertown, Massachusetts, won $120 from the Massachusetts Horticultural Society for devising "the most cheap and effective mode of destroying the rose-bug." His winning formula—though certainly simple—would be difficult to re-create today: "whale oil soap—2 pounds; water—15 gallons."

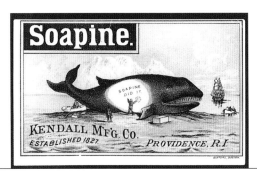

1842

The Great Hunger

Riding from Cork to Dublin on July 27, 1846, Father Mathew, a traveling priest, was reassured to see the potatoes blooming "in all luxuriance of an abundant harvest." The previous year's crop failure had caused unprecedented misery and death throughout Ireland, but these fields promised an end to the famine. Returning on the same road just one week later, however, Father Mathew's hopes were dashed. "I beheld with sorrow one wide waste of putrefying vegetation. In many places the wretched people were seated on the fences of their decaying gardens, wringing their hands." A fungus known as *Phytophthora infestans* was the immediate cause of the Irish potato famine; cruel and exploitative rule from London was a more fundamental reason. Nearly a million people died of starvation and disease. More than one and a half million fled the country.

1846

1847

Feeding the American Family

According to Robert Buist, a garden of about half an acre, sown with $10 worth of seeds, would supply "a moderate sized family with vegetables throughout the year." In *The Family Kitchen Gardener*, Buist gave practical advice to American gardeners who, he felt, relied too much on unsuitable Old World techniques. On the subject of fertilizer, Buist dismissed the modern weakness for gypsum and guano. For the very best manure, he contended, mix up horse, cow, and pig dung. "These, thrown into a heap to ferment, saturating it with all the

soapsuds and urine that can be collected, will form the best, the safest, and most permanent manure." In fact, Buist's advice—though delivered with an American accent—is sound old gardening lore. "Assiduity in the destruction of weeds, neatness and cleanliness, a constant stirring of the soil, digging deep and manuring freely, must be the constant companion of the gardener." Cato and Columella, those farming sages of ancient Rome, could not have said it better.

Weeds at Walden Pond

"That's Roman wormwood,—that's pigweed,—that's sorrel,— that's piper-grass,—have at him, chop him up, turn his roots upward to the sun." Henry David Thoreau was doing battle with the weeds in *Walden*, his classic account of the two years he spent living on Walden Pond (1845–47). "Daily the beans saw me come to the rescue armed with a hoe, and thin the ranks of their enemies, filling up the trenches with weeds dead." His great friend, neighbor, and fellow writer, Ralph Waldo Emerson, was not always so upbeat among the vegetables. Tending a garden kept one from doing anything else, he complained. "If a man owns land, the land owns him…the devotion to these vines and cornfields I find narrowing and poisonous." Emerson's tone sounds more like a lover's quarrel with his garden than like real resentment.

169

A Warm Welcome to Crabgrass

Crabgrass was not always the villain that it is today. In 1849 the U.S. Patent Office officially welcomed crabgrass into the country as a useful forage crop for America's hungry new population of domestic animals. People ate it, too. Crabgrass is a type of millet and was valued as a staple grain well into the twentieth century by immigrants from eastern Europe. But other crops outshone the hardy, unglamorous crabgrass, which soon lost its place on the American dinner menu. It took its revenge on the lawns of suburban America, long overstaying its once-warm welcome.

1850

The Virtues of a Vegetable Diet

In spite of the availability of meat and fish, a powerful vegetarian movement emerged in the United States during the middle years of the nineteenth century. Diseases, particularly among children, were depleting the population. In New York City, half of the children did not live to be six years old. Surely, reformers argued, their diet was responsible. Sylvester Graham (whose name is now enshrined in the Graham cracker, which he invented) preached vegetarianism, temperance, Christianity, and whole-meal flour. Dr. William Alcott—a cousin of Louisa May—opened America's first health-food store in Boston. In his inaugural address as president of the American Vegetarian Society (founded in 1850), Alcott revealed the responsibility that the humble carrot, potato, and bean were expected to shoulder: "A vegetable diet lies at the basis of all reform, whether civil, social, moral, or religious."

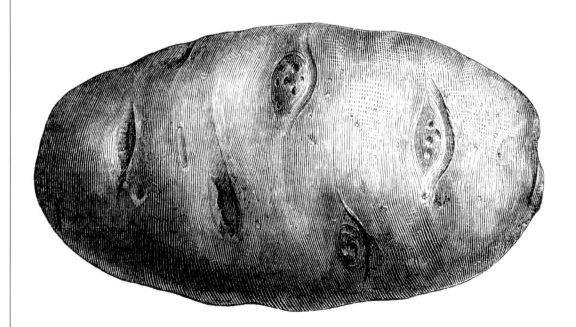

1851

Tomato Pills for Cholera

The English prejudice against the tomato was slow to die in the northern states. While southerners enthusiastically consumed tomatoes in sauces and soups, Yankees viewed these dishes with suspicion, some still clinging to the belief that tomatoes were poisonous. Surprisingly then, it was as a medicine that the tomato first impressed these skeptics. During the 1820s, word got around that the tomato could cure almost anything, including cholera—the epidemic killer that periodically swept through the swelling eastern cities. Promising "an antidote to contagious and epidemic diseases," manufacturers of tomato pills and extracts helped make the once-spurned vegetable acceptable. One remarkable statistic illustrates the tomato's rise: In all of 1833, only a single pound of tomato seed was sold in Boston; by 1851, yearly sales had risen to 1,000 pounds. A person could get addicted to tomatoes, suggested one Connecticut journal: "His family, if like the writer of this, will soon want their tomatoes—once—twice—three times a day, morning, noon, and evening!"

A Surfeit of Seeds

In 1800, Shaker merchants had plodded through the country, selling seeds from their wagons. Half a century later, the sale of seeds was a cutthroat industry. Catalogs became the fireside reading of the winter gardener, and there was a lot of information to digest. In its 1842 catalog, for instance, William R. Price listed 61 varieties of beans, 47 peas, and 30 turnips. In 1853, R. K. Bliss mailed out catalog orders from its Springfield, Massachusetts, headquarters. Bliss also led the way with color catalogs, which quickly became the only way to catch the attention of the increasingly befuddled gardener. Bliss listed 676 flower varieties in 1858; by 1865 that number had increased to 1,612. By the end of the century, around 800 seed companies were doing business in the United States. "Oh for the good old days when a strawberry was a strawberry and there was no perplexity about it," lamented one seed-saturated gardener.

Outdoing Versailles

Victorians gardeners loved a grand display of flowers and did not much mind if critics thought their taste a little crass. ("If you've got it, flaunt it," was how their philosophy might have been expressed 100 years later.) Imperialist plundering brought exotic new plants to England, and progress in glassmaking and steelmaking enabled the construction of huge greenhouses, making it easy for municipalities and landed gentry to raise colorful flowers by the thousands for planting in the early summer. Salvias, petunias, geraniums, lobelias, begonias, zinnias, and many other splashy bedding plants were densely set in geometric plots, allowing the public parks and private estates of Britain to look like garish parodies of Renaissance gardens. The park surrounding the Crystal Palace (a huge glass exhibition hall) in London was intended to outshine Versailles. The effect was dramatic, but not to everyone's liking. To William Robinson, an proponent of the natural look in gardens, the Crystal Palace extravaganza represented "the greatest modern example of the waste of enormous means in making hideous a fine piece of ground."

1856

Guano Obsession

One of the strangest chapters in gardening history was precipitated by guano, the nitrogen-rich droppings of seabirds. Farmers had discovered that when mixed with lime and loam, guano could quadruple a garden's output. Unfortunately for northern gardeners, Peru claimed many of the isolated islands where the treasured guano lay thickest. Determined to corner the world guano market, U.S. president Franklin Pierce pushed through the Guano Islands Act in 1856. This ordinance declared that any unclaimed island anywhere in the world would become the property of the United States if Americans occupied it first. The United States would claim more than 40 such islands before cheaper chemical fertilizers would diminish the nation's lust for bird droppings.

The Plant Hunters

Kew Gardens, London's great arboretum and center for botanical research, was a lively hub of exploration—and plant piracy—in Victorian Britain. Since its establishment in 1759, Kew had expanded from around 11 acres to more than 250. Botanists attached to Kew had combed the world's continents for plants that might prove commercially useful. Tea, rubber, and cinchona (the source of the antimalarial drug quinine) all found their way to the British Empire as a result of Kew's adventuring scientists. Chief among Kew's botanists was Joseph Hooker, who headed the gardens for 20 years, beginning in 1865. A tireless collector of plants himself, Hooker identified 303 new plant species, changing the landscape of Britain's gardens with 43 species of rhododendron.

The Pea Makes History

The pea's place in gardening history is enshrined by an Austrian monk named Gregor Mendel. When his bishop discouraged him from pursuing the "lewd" business of breeding animals, Mendel turned to growing peas—28,000 of them. "The bishop did not understand that plants also have sex," Mendel later explained. Based upon his observation of inherited traits in successive generations of peas, Mendel hypothesized the existence of dominant and recessive genes. His theory of heredity is still the basis of genetic science, but at the time no one was prepared to listen. "Experiments in Plant Hybridization," published in 1866, dropped into the sea of science without making a ripple. In 1900, this groundbreaking work was discovered, and Mendel was acclaimed the Father of Genetics. By then he had been dead for 16 years.

1866

Painting the Potatoes

Driven to desperation by the Colorado potato beetle (which had never feasted on potato plants until it found them growing in a frontier field), one farmer threw some leftover house paint over his infested crop. The insects rolled off the plants and died. So was born Paris Green, named after the arsenic-laced pigment in the paint. Its success spawned several other arsenic insecticides, including London Purple, a waste product of the carpet-dye industry. When sprayed or dusted in too-concentrated a formula, Paris Green killed the plants themselves; it was also death to bees. Farmers were so grateful to be free of pests that they chose not to consider arsenic's adverse toxic effects.

The Best of Both Worlds

The country was the healthy choice for bringing up one's family in mid-nineteenth-century America. Infant mortality rates for city children were nearly double those of their country cousins. But how could one keep a city job while enjoying the benefits of the country? The answer: Live in a newly built suburb and commute via railroad or perhaps by steam car along a tree-lined parkway. One of America's first communities specifically designed for the new "urban villagers" was Riverside, Illinois, just outside Chicago. The vision of landscape architect Frederick Law Olmsted (designer of New York's Central Park), Riverside incorporated curving streets and generous public space. Residents agreed not to build walls between their front lawns in order to create the effect of open parkland. Here, as in the many other new suburbs, the lawn mower became a permanent resident of the garden shed. "Whoever spends the early hours of one summer, while the dew spangles the grass, in pushing these grass-cutters over a velvety lawn. . .will never rest contented in the city," gushed one convert to suburbia.

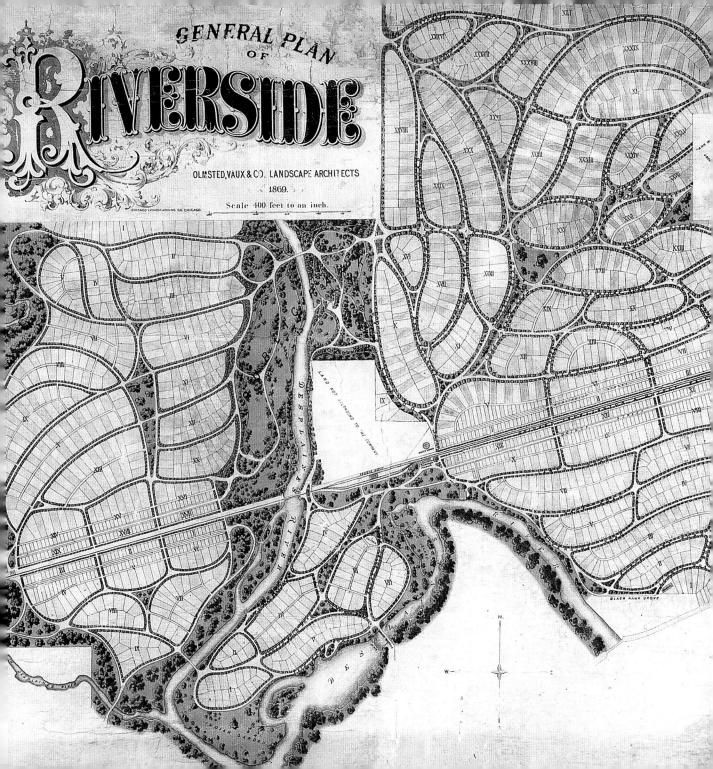

The Dawn of Silent Springs

Othmar Zeidler, a young German scientist, did not know what to do with the white powder he had created. Reacting chloral hydrate and chlorobenzene in the presence of sulfuric acid had resulted in a new compound, but to what purpose? Its name was certainly not a selling point. He put dichlorodiphenyl trichloroethane into storage and went on to other experiments. Sixty-five years later, renamed DDT, Zeidler's creation would launch a revolution—which would spur a counterrevolution—in insect control.

178

Growing a Bigger Onion

Few seedsmen harnessed the spirit of American enterprise as effectively as W. Atlee Burpee. The arrival of his huge catalog—free of charge and spectacularly illustrated—was an eagerly awaited event in the winter household. Burpee outspent the competition in advertising, and he outmaneuvered them in marketing. In 1882 he began offering prizes for the best and biggest fruits and vegetables grown from Burpee seeds. Under the "Mammoth Silver King Onion" in the 1888 catalog, for instance, Burpee typically challenged his readers: "We again offer, for 1888, CASH PRIZES OF $25.00 and $10.00 for the two largest onions raised from seed purchased of us this year." Burpee's entrepreneurial efforts had lasting effects; many of the varieties his catalogs introduced became gardening classics, including the 'Surehead' cabbage of 1877 and the ubiquitous 'Iceberg' lettuce of 1894.

1882

The "Planet Jr." No. 1
Combined Drill and
Wheel Hoe.

1897

The Wheel Hoe

The gas-powered rotary cultivator of the late twentieth century originated in the 1840s as the early wheel hoe. Single- or double-wheeled, these machines were pushed like lawnmowers and could be adapted to perform a variety of tasks, including plowing, raking, cultivating, and seed drilling. By the end of the nineteenth century, a wheel hoe was in the barn or shed of every up-to-date gardener. It was "the most important garden tool invented within a century," claimed *Garden Magazine* in 1905. The 1897 *Sears, Roebuck Catalogue* offered eight models of wheel hoe (versus seven conventional hand hoes). These ranged from the "Fire Fly" at $2 ("very useful to plow up the chicken yards") to the "Planet Jr. No. 1" at $9 ("without equal in variety of tools, easy adjustment, lightness, strength, and beauty"). Nearly a century later, the wheel hoe would be reintroduced as the "latest" product for the environmentally friendly gardener.

A Champion for the Cottage Garden

After nearly a century of flirting with exotic shrubs and showy bedding flowers, English gardeners discovered that there was no place like home. Foxgloves, meadowsweets, Canterbury bells, hollyhocks, and delphiniums—which had quietly adorned cottage gardens since medieval days—triumphantly emerged as antidotes to Victorian vulgarity. And one of their most eloquent advocates was Gertrude Jekyll (1843–1932), who brought an artist's eye for color and form to her designs for long-blooming herbaceous borders. "I have learned much from the little cottage gardens that help to make our English waysides the prettiest in the temperate world," wrote Jekyll in *Wood and Garden*, one of her many books that fondly recalled a tranquil, preindustrial age.

New Hues in the Rose Garden

While empires expanded, wars raged, and workers rebelled, the rose growers of Europe and America sought to resolve an age-old human problem: Is it possible to capture the bright yellow of the Persian wild rose in a hybrid perpetual, which bloomed all season long? After years of painstaking cross-breeding, a Frenchman named Joseph Pernet-Ducher finally came up with fertile seeds. His 'Soleil d'Or', introduced to the world in 1900, was a major breakthrough in rose breeding. From this yellow hybrid evolved a new range of long-lasting colors in the rose gardener's palette: golds, bright corals, hot pinks, and vivid oranges.

| 1900

1909

Famous Last Words

The U.S. Bureau of Soils was not alarmed by pessimistic agriculturists who warned that America's humus-depleted farmland was beginning to blow away. Official governmental policy held that poor soil was like an empty tank; all you had to do was fill it up with the right balance of chemicals, and fertility would magically return. "The soil is the one indestructible, immutable asset that the nation possesses," announced the Bureau with almost comic inaccuracy in 1909. "It is the one resource that cannot be exhausted; that cannot be used up." Many believed that tired American topsoil would be replenished with the application of a few miracle fertilizers—a position held by some modern fertilizer manufacturers.

1911

Bacteria Enter the Battle—Slowly

At the height of the enthusiasm for chemical pesticides, scientists in the German province of Thuringia isolated a bacterium that would become a significant player in the organic control of insects. When eaten by a cabbageworm or other susceptible larva, *Bacillus thuringiensis* (or BT, as it came to be known) multiplies rapidly, eventually killing its host. Like that other alphabetical killer, DDT, BT waited for years on the laboratory shelf before reaching the crops. Not until 1958 would BT become available commercially in the United States.

The War Years

In the first half of the twentieth century, the world went to war as it had never before. Inspired by new knowledge about the nature of matter, chemists devised weapons of mass destruction. Leaders dealt in death as if killing were a game, taking down millions of innocent bystanders. There seemed no end to the carnage. And the picture was even more grim *outside* the garden.

In fact, garden philosophy and world politics did share a macabre set of values during the decades that began the twentieth century. Might was right, in the garden as on the battlefield. Those who held the weapons felt entitled to obliterate whatever was inconvenient.

Weeds and insects fell to the onslaught of untested toxins, along with the birds and the bees, the farm laborers, the children playing by the side of the field, and a not a few unsuspecting consumers. Humanity had surrendered any sense of stewardship in exchange for the intoxicating illusion of absolute dominion.

Look a little closer, though, and the picture was not so bleak. There were, as there always have been, dedicated gardeners for whom growing and harvesting is an act of kinship with the living world. And there were a few who dedicated themselves to finding an alternative to reckless science. Just as the worst nightmares were materializing, the realization began to emerge that humans could live and prosper in harmony with nature.

1916

Japanese beetles are found on shrubs in New Jersey.

1914

Terrorists assassinate Austrian archduke Francis Ferdinand and the duchess of Hohenberg. Austria declares war on Serbia, and World War I begins.

1922

The USSR forms.

1920

American horse population wanes, and garden manure is scarce.

1922

Beatrix Farrand designs gardens at Dumbarton Oaks.

1915

Liberty Hyde Bailey writes of nature's intrinsic value and humans' responsibility to learn about and care for the earth.

1918

Victory gardeners conserve resources and plant front-yard food crops for victory.

1921

George Washington Carver testifies to the usefulness of the peanut.

1924

Rudolph Steiner rejects modern agricultural shortcuts, advocating the wonders of his biodynamic method.

1929

The New York stock market crashes, launching the Great Depression.

1932

Duke Ellington writes the Big Band hit "It Don't Mean a Thing (If It Ain't Got That Swing)."

1923

Blues singer Bessie Smith records "Down-hearted Blues."

Adolf Hitler writes *Mein Kampf.*

1927

Virginia Woolf writes *To the Lighthouse.*

1930

Vita Sackville-West and Harold Nicolson plant wildly at Sissinghurst Castle.

1933

Consumers worry about arsenic and lead in their food.

Adolf Hitler becomes the chancellor of Germany and leader of the Third Reich.

1939

Paul Müller uses DDT as an insecticide, later earning a Nobel Prize.

World War II begins.

1941

Orson Welles directs *Citizen Kane.*

1943

Some gardeners are victorious, but Ogden Nash mourns his pathetic victory garden.

Max Newman and T. H. Flowers invent the electronic computer.

1946

Trumpeter and band leader Dizzy Gillespie writes "A Night In Tunisia."

The first United Nations General Assembly is held in London, with representatives from 51 countries attending.

1940

An Agricultural Testament, by Sir Albert Howard, is published. Howard asks farmers and gardeners to forsake chemicals and to study composting.

1942

J. I. Rodale publishes *Organic Farming and Gardening* out of concern for the world's health.

1945

The 'Peace' rose is named.

The United States drops atomic bombs on the Japanese cities of Hiroshima and Nagasaki.

1948

Fairfield Osborn writes of humanity's conflict with nature.

Israel becomes an independent Jewish state.

1953

Joseph Stalin dies.

1959

A World War II chemical weapon, parathion, is used on farms—and destroys more than insects.

Cranberries from Washington and Oregon are ordered off the market because of contamination by the chemical weed killer aminotriazole.

1952

Scholars and the national media underestimate organic gardening.

The United States performs its first nuclear bomb test on the Eniwetok Atoll in the Pacific.

1957

Ghana becomes a nation.

1958

The United States launches the first space satellite, Explorer I.

The laser is invented.

Squirt Gun Soldiers

No one voiced the new ambivalence of humanity's role in the natural world as clearly as Liberty Hyde Bailey (1858–1954). A professor at Cornell University, he was for decades America's preeminent horticulturist, an inspiring teacher, and the author of 66 books and 700 scholarly papers. He both loved the earth and marched to the drumbeat of modern science. As editor of *American Garden*, he spoke of the backyard as a battlefield: "In your generation and mine men must shoulder their squirt guns as our ancestors shouldered their muskets, " he wrote. In his book *The Holy Earth*—one of the cornerstones of the movement known today as "deep ecology"—he wrote with lyrical affection for the planet: "Verily then, the earth is divine because man did not make it…. We are under obligation to take part and to do our best, living with each other and with all creatures." While Bailey's views may seem contradictory, no one can dispute the principal upon which he based his opinions. Only knowing "the facts of the earth," Bailey contended, would enable us to solve its problems.

Introducing *Popillia Japonica*

No one noticed the little gray-white grubs that clung to the soil around the roots of imported Japanese shrubs in late 1915. The following summer a few adult *Popillia japonica* emerged from the ground to feast on the shrubs near Riverton, New Jersey. The glossy brown immigrants—known as Japanese beetles—encountered no natural enemies in their new environment. They spread like a plague over the gardens of the eastern United States. One scientist in 1923 described filling "in somewhat less than two hours" 13 barrels—each with a capacity of 16 gallons—with beetles shaken from an orchard of peach trees. "The next morning," he added despairingly, "the beetles were apparently as numerous on these trees as before." Since those early years of the struggle, *Popillia japonica* has become a permanent resident, subdued but not vanquished.

Digging for Victory

"Whenever I see a man make a bonfire these days without having a piece of tin sheeting or some old tub under it to catch the ash, I feel like shouting at him 'stop that waste.' " Like most American gardeners during the spring of 1918, this writer was up in arms over the war effort. Fear of food shortages, combined with genuine patriotic impulses, had turned even the most indolent householders to gardening. Golf courses, public parks, and front lawns were given over to corn and potatoes. President Woodrow Wilson solemnly urged self-sacrifice: "Everyone who creates or cultivates a garden helps…. This is a time for America to correct her unpardonable fault of wastefulness and extravagance." Self-sacrifice came to an end later that same year, with the Armistice of November 11.

1918

193

Where Have All the Horses Gone?

"How thoroughly the automobile has displaced the city horse!" commented *The Garden Magazine*. Between 1900 and 1920, the writer observed, the urban population of New York State had increased from 5.5 to 8.5 million. During the same time period, the state's horse population had decreased from 300,000 to less than half that number. With each horse producing an estimated 22 pounds of manure per day, this caused a significant drop in the stores of garden fertilizer. "As a result," continued the article, there were "no more loads upon loads of manure drawn from the city." In two decades, the problem of how to dispose of excess manure had changed to a problem of how to get enough manure. Composting and crop rotation were viable alternatives to manuring, but in an age when science seemed to have all the agricultural answers, gardeners increasingly chose the chemical option.

1920

Peanut Rubber

The peanut and the sweet potato found an inventive advocate in George Washington Carver. Don't just eat them, urged Carver, make glue, or flour, or wood filler out of them. Born to slave parents near the end of the Civil War, Carver earned a master's degree in botany at Iowa State College, then went on to Tuskegee Research Institute in Alabama, where he devoted a lifetime to promoting the welfare of rural Southerners, encouraging them to improve their soil and to create useful products out of their most common crops. In Carver's fertile mind, the peanut, sweet potato, soybean, and pecan became the building blocks of industry.

"This Grand Art of Mine"

In the man's world of landscape architecture, Beatrix Farrand (1872–1959) moved with perfect confidence at the very top of her profession. As a wealthy only child in New York City, she might have been expected to flutter through Manhattan's social calendar for a year or two before settling down to marriage. Instead, she devoted her debutante days to traveling and self-improvement. In the Renaissance gardens of Italy she discovered the beauty of symmetry; in the country gardens of England she fell in love with the exuberant natural plantings of Gertrude Jekyll and William Robinson. She carried these influences with her through a lifetime of private and public commissions, including work for Princeton and Yale Universities. In 1922, at Dumbarton Oaks, the Washington, D.C., estate of Robert and Mildred Bliss, she began work on one of her most admired creations. Later she elegantly modified these designs when the gardens passed to the ownership of Harvard University. With gardens such as Dumbarton Oaks as her living monuments, Farrand is remembered as one of the most dedicated and inspired of American gardeners. "With this grand art of mine," she told *The New York Herald Tribune* early in her career, "I do not envy the greatest painter, or sculptor or poet that lived."

In 1921 Carver achieved national celebrity after testifying about peanuts before a congressional committee. Suddenly, mainstream America became aware of peanut milk, salad oil, and facial cream. Thomas Edison, it is said, was so impressed that he offered Carver a six-figure salary (which Carver refused). Of the hundreds of uses Carver dreamed up for southern produce, this humble man is best remembered not for the synthetic rubber, instant coffee, insulating board, wood stains, or shaving cream he developed, but for promoting that gooey mortar of American society: peanut butter.

Magic in the Manure Pile

Not everyone subscribed to the chemical formulas of agricultural science. An early protest came from Rudolph Steiner (1861–1925), the Austrian philosopher who founded the spiritual movement anthroposophy. In 1924, combining science and mysticism, Steiner outlined his system of biodynamic farming. Everything is interdependent, Steiner maintained. The best farms are self-sustaining, recycling products and working with the rhythms of nature. But Steiner went beyond rejecting the solutions of modern science. He held that the moon and stars influenced all growing things. Even more unusual were his composting methods. Steiner formulated rituals for adding key ingredients to the manure pile; yarrow flower should be placed in the bladder of a red deer stag, then left hanging in the sun for the summer before burial for the winter. Only then should it be added to compost. Biodynamics won many converts, and its followers still farm according to Steiner's exacting principles.

From the Rocks to the Flowerbeds

The marriage of writer Vita Sackville-West and Harold Nicolson started on the rocks and ended among England's most admired flowerbeds. Their early relationship—remembered mainly for bisexual scandals—was the talk of literary London. But after purchasing Sissinghurst Castle, this wealthy couple evolved into a renowned gardening partnership. With Harold as principal designer and Vita in charge of planting, the pair began work on Sissinghurst in 1930, harnessing his sense of structure to her love of profusion. "There should be the strictest formality of design, with the maximum informality of planting," explained Vita, who confessed a love for the "wildly unsymmetrical mess" of English cottage gardens. Whatever their secret, the magic worked. Years after Vita and Harold's deaths, Sissinghurst would remain one of Britain's most beautiful and popular estates, and its ethereal White Garden would be much visited and widely imitated.

100,000,000 Guinea Pigs

Public outrage against the use of insecticides is nothing new. A lively consumer movement arose in the 1930s, inflamed by the dangers of arsenic and lead residues on fruits and vegetables. "Willing or not, if you eat apples, pears, cherries, and berries, celery, and other fruit and vegetables, you are also eating arsenic," wrote the authors of a 1933 bestseller entitled *100,000,000 Guinea Pigs*, a title that referred to consumers' unwitting ingestion of toxic substances. As always, children were the ones who were most vulnerable to toxins in the diet. As a 1937 publication memorably pointed out:

> *Any bug that eats lead*
> *Will soon need a casket;*
> *Children should skin*
> *The fruit in the basket.*

| 1933

DDT to the Rescue!

Not all of America's wartime enemies were human. The Pacific's malarial mosquito and typhus-carrying louse in Italy were also dreaded foes. To the rescue came a secret weapon, a compound that had been sitting on a shelf since 1874. Used as an insecticide in 1939 by Swiss chemist Paul Müller (who would win a Nobel Prize for his work), DDT served on the front line of U.S. military action. When sprayed as an oil over Pacific islands before troops landed, it wiped out millions of mosquitoes. When dusted on a soldier, it annihilated lice. "It is the War's greatest contribution to the future health of the world," said Brigadier General James Simmons.

Unlike many weapons, DDT was not decommissioned after the war. If it could do such a job on mosquitoes and lice, imagine what wonders it would do in gardens. "The army's new insect-killer has nearly every householder pawing the ground in eagerness," reported one magazine. A few voices protested, but the desire for a miracle was too great to curb the gardening and farming public. It would be more than 25 years before the effects of DDT's long-lasting toxicity would be fully understood, and the war hero driven from its land.

1939 |

Reforming the Manure Heap

"All over the world our capital is being squandered," warned Sir Albert Howard. The reader in 1940 might have had visions of another stock market crash, but it was not economic doom that Howard feared, as his next sentence made clear: "The restoration and maintenance of soil fertility has become a universal problem."

While working as a botanist in India, Howard came to realize that only traditional composting methods could maintain the essential microorganisms of the soil. He set out his ideas in *The Waste Products of Agriculture* (1931), following this up with *An Agricultural Testament* (1940), the work that brought him fame—and considerable notoriety. "The slow poisoning of the life of the soil by artificial manures is one of the greatest calamities which has befallen agriculture and mankind," he argued. The solution: "Reform the manure heap—the weakest link in Western agriculture." Abandoning chemicals and studying the science of composting would lead to healthier crops, animals, and people, he concluded. While many agricultural experts and administrators dismissed Howard as a crackpot, an alert few took his analysis seriously. Among them was the young J. I. Rodale, whose exposure to Howard's *Testament* led to the birth of America's organic gardening movement.

Apostle of Organic Gardening

Nothing about Jerome I. Rodale's early years suggested that he would become the leader of America's organic gardening movement. As a Manhattan boy with poor health and weak eyesight, he grew a few flowers on his Lower East Side fire escape. Later he worked as a tax auditor. Teaming up with his brother in a successful electrical equipment business, J. I. (as he was known) made enough money to start his own publishing company in Emmaus, Pennsylvania. His particular interest in the subject of human health led him to the work of Sir Albert Howard—and to an epiphany: Healthy, humus-rich soil would grow healthy crops and promote improved public health. "His idea hit me like a ton of bricks," J. I. wrote of the experience.

This inspired formula launched J. I. Rodale on a stubborn campaign that would profoundly influence the face of American gardening. In 1942 he published the first 12-page edition of *Organic Farming and Gardening*, dropping "Farming" from the title when it became clear that his most enthusiastic readers were the victory gardeners and backyard enthusiasts of city and suburb. In 1947 J. I. established the Soil and Health Foundation, a research and education center later renamed the Rodale Institute. J. I. died in 1971, but his family has carried on his hard work. His visionary movement to improve the health of humanity by caring for the soil shows no sign of flagging in the third millennium.

Digging for Victory II

Would you like a description of my parsley?

I can give it to you in one word—gharsley!

Even Ogden Nash, it seems, had caught the victory garden bug. Americans had once again turned their rooftops, window boxes, and spare lots into kitchen gardens. At Eleanor Roosevelt's urging, cabbages, tomatoes, carrots, and beans grew on the White House lawn. To a government call for 18 million victory gardens, Americans responded with more than 21 million, producing an estimated 40 percent of all U.S. vegetables. "Many enjoyed, for the first time in their lives, the health that comes from working on the land, the satisfaction of seeing seed grow into plant," enthused *House and Garden* magazine in 1943. Not so Ogden Nash, whose garden was a back-breaking failure:

Do you wonder then, that my arteries harden

Whenever I think of my Victory Garden?

1945

'Peace' in Our Time

The most popular rose of the modern era began life as part of the Meilland nursery in France, bearing the unmemorable name of "3-35-40." In 1939, just before World War II, the Meillands managed to distribute cuttings to growers in Germany, Italy, and the United States—proving that rose breeding transcends politics. It was a spectacular flower of the hybrid tea group, with creamy yellow petals giving way to pink at the tips. In 1945, on the day that Berlin fell, 3-35-40 received its official name at a ceremony in California. "We are persuaded," said the organizers, "that this greatest new rose of our time should be named for the world's greatest desire, *peace*." Later that year, delegates at the first meeting of the United Nations each received a single blossom. "May it help to move all men of goodwill to strive for Peace on earth for all mankind," read the accompanying note.

1948

The Continuing Conflict

"When is a vegetable not a vegetable?" When the soil that produces it is impoverished, answered Fairfield Osborn in *Our Plundered Planet*. Osborne's 1948 blast at man's inhumanity to Mother Nature was one of the first books to suggest that the continued greedy exploitation of the earth would bring an end to civilization. A terrible world war had ended, wrote Osborne, but another cruel war still raged on more quietly. "This other world-wide war, still continuing, is bringing more widespread distress to the human race than any that have resulted from armed conflict. . . . This other war is man's conflict with nature."

1952

"Organic Farming—Bunk!"

By the 1950s, the growing number of converts to traditional, organic garden-ing was clearly beginning to make the experts nervous. *Horticulture* magazine

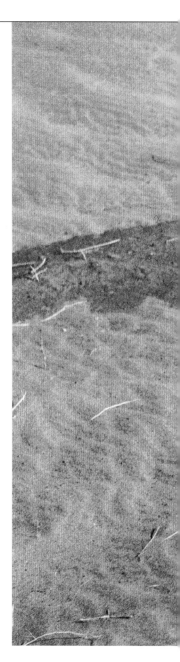

took the high road in politely putting down what it called "This 'Organic Gardening' Business." There simply is not enough organic material in the world to replace chemical fertilizers, argued Ray Koon of the University of Massachusetts. "And we don't relish the thought of starving to death," he added. Such understatement was not the style of *The Reader's Digest*. "Organic Farming—Bunk!" it bellowed in 1952.

1959

Weapons of Destruction

To many farmers and gardeners, a poison as quick and lethal as parathion was wasted on mere insects. In 1959, irritated by birds attacking their corn, farmers in Indiana killed an estimated 65,000 blackbirds and starlings in a single aerial attack. But parathion took its toll on people, too. More than 200 cases of parathion

poisoning were reported annually in California alone, while in Japan the poison claimed an average of 336 lives per year. Such figures would not have surprised the German chemists who developed a group of organic phosphates, including parathion, for use against human beings during the Second World War.

The Past Meets the Future

"My God! I beat a man insensible with a strawberry!" gasps Woody Allen in a scene from *Sleeper*, a futurist farce set in the year 2173. When the film was made in 1973, the idea of scientists transforming fruits and vegetables into monstrosities was simply a joke. Today, however, some wonder where Woody Allen bought his crystal ball.

The history of gardening in the late twentieth century can be compared to a tug of war. Pulling from one side are environmentalists, ethicists, and lovers of a simpler life, who fear that technology and industry are in danger of careening out of control. At times these activists have seemed to prevail. Environmentalism is no longer a dirty word. (The adjective "green" will sell almost anything.) The use of DDT in the United States was stopped in its tracks—although it is still used in many other countries. Traditional gardening practices are out of the closet. Organic produce is available in major supermarkets.

Look at the forces pulling in the other direction, however, and all bets are off. Spurred by scientific curiosity, genuine philanthropy, and pure greed, the leaders of technology and agribusiness empty their coffers into the pockets of obliging politicians. It is a powerful partnership. In that faraway field in 2173, who will be growing the strawberries, and how?

1962

Rachel Carson writes *Silent Spring,* which will become a bestseller.

1969

U.S. astronauts land on Earth's moon.

1966

Mao Zedong's Cultural Revolution begins in China.

Stalking the Wild Asparagus, by Euell Gibbons, offers advice on foraging for wild foods.

Einstein writes *The Meaning of Relativity.*

1965

Malcolm X writes *The Autobiography of Malcolm X.*

IBM invents the word processor.

1970

The first Earth Day is celebrated.

1967

The U.N. Food and Agriculture Organization calls for increased use of Integrated Pest Management techniques.

1971

The Maine Organic Farmers and Gardeners Association bands together to promote organics.

1973

Fifty farmers organize California Certified Organic Farmers.

1975

The Seed Savers Exchange is founded to preserve plant diversity.

1974

John Jeavons praises the benefits of raised beds and intensive gardening.

Permaculture thrives at Bill Mollison's Permaculture Research Institute in New South Wales, Australia.

The Aztecs' staple crop amaranth is rediscovered—and is lauded for its nutritional value.

1977

Nelson Mandela gardens in prison.

1972

DDT use is banned in the United States. Eagle, osprey, and peregrine falcon populations begin to recover.

1980

Paul Berg receives a Nobel Prize for his work in recombinant DNA, which will change the agricultural world.

The first U.S. patent for a genetically engineered organism, a bacterium used to clean up oil spills, is granted.

1984

Community gardens flourish in U.S. inner cities.

1989

Prince Charles tries his hand at organic farming.

1981

The Rodale Institute Farming Systems Trial begins. The trial will demonstrate that in years with low amounts of rainfall, organic farms out-produce farms that use chemicals.

The AIDS virus is officially recognized by the Centers for Disease Control and Prevention.

1986

An accident occurs at a nuclear plant in Chernobyl, USSR.

1990

The U.S. Department of Agriculture begins the struggle to define standards for organics.

1995

Alice Waters starts the Edible Schoolyard and gets kids gardening.

2000

Studies report that gardening is hard work and good exercise. Gardeners are not exactly shocked.

1998

Russian families garden for survival, producing 90 percent of the country's potato crop.

1991

Arizona's Biosphere 2 is built.

1999

Monsanto Corporation introduces a way to produce infertile seeds.

Research shows that organic soybean and corn crops absorb greenhouse gases.

New BT corn kills garden pests...and monarch butterflies.

1997

Ian Wilmut clones a sheep.

1994

The 'Flavr Savr' tomato, the first genetically engineered food, goes on sale in supermarkets.

"And No Bird Sings"

"What has already silenced the voices of spring in countless towns in America? This book is an attempt to explain." Rachel Carson was not the first writer to warn about the dangers of pesticides, but in *Silent Spring* she combined an ecologist's scientific authority with the passion and lyricism of a poet. The book caught the public's attention and marked the beginning of the modern environmental movement. "As crude a weapon as the cave man's club, the chemical barrage has been hurled against the fabric of life," wrote Carson, and with those words, DDT's days were numbered. But her message was not one just for the moment. The larger theme of Carson's *Silent Spring* is still essential to heed: "The 'control of nature,' " she wrote, "is a phrase conceived in arrogance, born of the Neanderthal age of biology and philosophy, when it was supposed that nature exists for the convenience of man."

Managing the Pests

In a world damaged by its own technology and humanity's love affair with the idea of progress, opposition to chemical pesticides was growing within the establishment itself. Official organizations increasingly called for a more measured reliance on poisons. Why not attack the pests on all fronts—with predators and parasites, natural diseases, crop rotation, resistant varieties, environmental modification, and mechanical traps, using poisons only as a fallback? The idea was not new. Sensible gardeners had been practicing such holistic methods for years. But this new approach to pest control finally had a name: Integrated Pest Management, or IPM for short. The United Nations Food and Agriculture Organization was one of the first groups to define it in 1967. By 1979, U.S. president Jimmy Carter was openly calling for action, instructing governmental agencies "to support and adopt IPM strategies wherever practicable."

the
past
meets
the
future

215

1970

Earth Gets a Day

Earth Day didn't just happen—it erupted, bursting onto our holiday schedule on April 22, 1970, with lectures, bike-ins, hikes, eco-tours, demonstrations, and stunts such as Miami's Dead Orange Parade, which awarded prizes to the "most polluted" floats. "It is nothing short of incredible," gasped Wisconsin senator Gaylord Nelson, Earth Day's official founder, who, only seven months earlier, had proposed a national day to mark

environmental awareness. The euphoric energy of the 1970s did not last. Earth Day did. The event became an annual celebration of spring, even if increasingly co-opted by the establishment it had once decried. By the late 1990s, according to one poll, two-thirds of Americans considered themselves "actively pro-environment," and only 4 percent admitted to being "unsympathetic" to environmental issues.

Pitching Politics—And Manure

Environmentalism was in the air when the Maine Organic Farmers and Gardeners Association (MOFGA) first began addressing the needs of alternative farmers around the state. But this was no back-to-nature hobby for organic flower children; these hippies had teeth. Thirty years later—with 200 certified growers and 3,000 members, a quarterly newspaper, and even its own radio call-in show—MOFGA boasted a string of environmental achievements and exerted a political and social influence in the state matched by few such organizations in the country. In 1997 MOFGA pushed through the passage of a bill requiring all state agencies "to promote the principles of integrated pest management and other science-based technology to minimize reliance on pesticides." That same year, Maine became the first state to ban corn that was genetically engineered to incorporate BT poisons. Life was not all outreach and lobbying, however. At the annual Common Ground Country Fair, MOFGA's major fund-raising event, visitors could enjoy fine food, crafts, and music, as well as a chance to witness the Harry S. Truman Memorial Manure Pitch-Off.

The Eagle Soars Back

How could American agriculture survive without its most cherished poison? (A ban would result in "the end of all human progress," claimed one industry spokesman.) By 1972, however, a tidal wave of grassroots opposition—set in motion by Rachel Carson's *Silent Spring*—finally ended DDT's use in the United States. The irrefutable proof that America's own national symbol, the bald eagle, was facing extinction (along with ospreys, peregrine falcons, brown pelicans, and countless other birds) led to the Environmental Protection Agency's historic decision. The effects were dramatic. Between 1963 and 1996, the number of breeding pairs of bald eagles in the lower 48 states increased from fewer than 500 pairs to more than 5,000. The 39 pairs of breeding peregrine falcons (who were limited to the western states in 1975) increased to nearly 1,000, including a regular couple on the ledge of Boston's old Custom House tower. The lesson, according to activist Barry Commoner, was to attack pollutants at the point of origin. "If you don't put something into the environment," he wrote, "it isn't there."

Size Is *Not* Important

Is it possible to feed a person for a year on just 700 square feet of land? Could a gardener make a livable income on as little as one-eighth of an acre? These were the questions that a former systems analyst named John Jeavons set out to answer in his California gardens. Along the way, he convinced a lot of people that intensive gardening in raised beds, a system derived from the biodynamic methods of Rudolph Steiner, could produce harvests many times greater than the national average.

His 1974 bestseller, *How to Grow More Vegetables (Than You Ever Thought Possible on Less Land Than You Can Imagine)*, showed how to transform postage-stamp backyards into productive kitchen gardens. More important to the visionary Jeavons, who saw the loss of topsoil as one of the world's most urgent and neglected problems: The book was adopted as a much-loved text in parts of rural India.

"We Need a Lot More Gardeners"

"In order to change our ways, we seem to need to terrify ourselves," wrote Bill Mollison. The earth, he warned, was literally wasting away under the reckless assaults of industrial agriculture. Unlike many critics of modern farming, however, the Tasmanian-born Mollison had a vigorous and practical solution. In 1974, after a checkered career of shark hunting, cattle running, wildlife biology, university study, teaching, and dancehall bouncing, Mollison, along with his colleague David Holmgren, developed the principles of permaculture, a self-sustaining agricultural system that is based, as he put it, on "a philosophy of working with rather than against nature."

Permaculture has three tenets: "care of the earth," "care of people," and "setting limits to population and consumption." Mollison's system "arranges what was always there in a different way…to conserve energy or to generate more energy than it consumes." Students at the Permaculture Research Institute home base, the 147-acre Tagari Farm, in New South Wales, Australia, learn forest gardening, aquaculture, nontillage agriculture, and water conservation. Mollison aims to educate an international corps of farmers to work on a small scale—the only efficient way to farm. "We need a lot more gardeners," he wrote. "Gardeners are the most productive, most hands-on sort of agriculturalists. They always have been."

1974

The Fall and Rise of Amaranth

To sixteenth-century Spanish priests in the New World, the Aztec ceremonies they witnessed were pure sacrilege. They watched in astonishment as temple maidens created a huge image of the war god Huizilopochtli from a paste of amaranth and maize flour. Worse was to come. After parades and celebrations, the Aztecs offered human sacrifices to their image, then proceeded to break apart and eat their god in a spirit of devotion. For this and similar examples of idolatry, in 1525 the Catholic Church began to suppress all Aztec religious practices. Amaranth, which had been one of the staple foods of the Aztec Empire, declined in prestige, becoming the peasants' food of Mexico.

Centuries later, nutritionists and anthropologists rediscovered this nutritious and versatile grain, which is more protein-rich than wheat, maize, or rice. In 1974, Rodale's Organic Gardening and Farming Research Center began a study of the ancient cereal, and soon the "news" of its nutritional value spread. Before long the showy red, purple, and green flowers of amaranth were adding a splash of color to the golden wheat country of America's West. Ground and flattened into cereal flakes, amaranth is once again part of a North American ritual—this time not as a dietary staple, nor as a part of ancient ceremonies, but instead, as another twentieth-century wonder: instant breakfast.

Living History

Diane Whealy's family had saved and grown seeds from one purple morning glory for over a century. A handful of these seeds inspired Whealy and her husband, Kent, to found the Seed Savers Exchange. Striving to preserve the diversity of traditional vegetables, fruits, and flowers neglected by the major seed companies, the Whealys established a network of backyard farmers with a passion for the vanishing heirloom varieties. Twenty-five years later, there were 8,000 active Seed Savers Exchange members keeping America's gardening heritage alive by exchanging and growing seeds not available from conventional catalogs. On their own 170-acre Heritage Farm in Iowa, the Whealys have maintained around 18,000 varieties of fruit and garden plants, including an amazing 4,000 types of tomatoes and nearly 500 apples. For his pioneering work in maintaining biodiversity, Kent Whealy received a MacArthur "genius" grant in 1990.

Gardening behind Bars

"To survive in prison, one must develop ways to take satisfaction in one's daily life," wrote South Africa's most illustrious prisoner. While serving a life sentence on an island near Cape Town, Nelson Mandela cultivated a stony strip of earth in the prison courtyard and began to grow vegetables. "The authorities did not regret giving permission, for once the garden began to flourish, I often provided the wardens with some of my best tomatoes and onions," he wrote in his autobiography.

When manual labor came to an end for prisoners in 1977, Mandela devoted more time to his prison vegetable patch, ordering books on gardening and horticulture. The garden prospered. Only the peanuts, Mandela confessed, consistently failed. "I saw the garden as a metaphor for certain aspects of my life. A leader must also tend his garden; he, too, plants seeds, and then watches, cultivates, and harvests the results." In 1990, after 27 years in prison, Mandela was finally free to cultivate the larger land to which he had devoted his life.

the
past
meets
the
future

The Dawn of Biotechnology

Dr. Paul Berg received his Nobel Prize for chemistry in 1980, long before the average gardener had heard even a whisper about genetic engineering. His work in recombinant DNA—a technique to splice a gene of one organism into the DNA of another—led to a field that has subsequently revolutionized world agriculture. From the outset, Berg was aware of the dangers inherent in the new technology. He called for a moratorium on the technique, convening a meeting at which 100 scientists met to discuss the physical and ethical problems biotechnology might encounter. The National Institutes of Health guidelines, published in 1976, released the new discipline to universities and industry. Eighteen years later a new tomato, the 'Flavr Savr', would appear in supermarkets. The rest is biotech history.

226

1984

Greening the Cities

Not everyone with a hankering for a better life went back to the country. In many American cities—devastated by neglect and reckless development—local residents began taking charge of their own environments. They cleared spare lots and abandoned parks, shipped in soil, and constructed walkways and raised beds. The community garden movement revitalized many run-down neighborhoods, giving older people a place to relax, the young valuable recreation, and many families a first taste of truly fresh vegetables. A survey of New York City by the Neighborhood Open Space Coalition in 1984 discovered that 11,171 people were tending 448 community gardens on a total of 155 acres. More than half of these plots were cultivated using low-chemical or organic methods. "It is like giving birth to a baby," said one city gardener, of the community gardeners' creative hard work. "Anything we could make come alive we have done so."

Prince of Compost

In the midst of his tabloid-tragic marriage to Princess Diana, Britain's Prince Charles made a bold decision. Having experimented successfully with growing crops organically on 85 acres of his Gloucestershire estate, he decided to commit the whole of his Home Farm (more than 1,000 acres) to organic agriculture. "The 'experts' were very nice to me in my presence," wrote Charles—who was widely regarded at the time as a crank—but he suspected that behind his back they were scoffing at "this latest demonstration of insanity." In fairy-tale fashion, however, the prince's organic venture was an environmental and commercial success. Worms returned to the refreshed soil; weeds diminished with careful management. And organic products under the Duchy Originals brand began selling out at the supermarkets. "In farming, as in gardening," wrote the not-so-cranky prince, "I happen to believe that if you treat the land with love and respect…then it will repay you in kind."

Defining Organic

People had been growing organic produce for decades, but what exactly did the word organic mean? Some states had their own specifications; many had none. Wouldn't a nationally accepted definition for organic food ease interstate commerce and satisfy confused consumers? With this worthy objective in mind, in 1990 the U.S. Department of Agriculture assembled a 14-member board to identify the new organic standards. A glance at the conflicting interests represented on the panel—environmentalists, scientists, consumer advocates, and food-industry representatives—suggested heated debate in the years to come, but few observers could have foreseen the firestorm of controversy that would erupt when the committee finally delivered its conclusions.

the
past
meets
the
future

229

| 1990

Seven long years later, in 1997, the USDA-proposed guidelines for defining organic food went over like a transgenic rutabaga. Not only did the 600-page document suggest that both irradiating food and fertilizing with sewage sludge fell neatly within the definition of organic, but it also opened its generous embrace to genetically modified crops. The response from the American public was a noisy, organic raspberry. The National Organic Standards Board found its Web site choked with hostile messages. The proposals retreated back to committee. In December 2000 the USDA would adopt stricter standards for food labeled as organic; antibiotics, irradiation, sewage sludge, and synthetic fertilizers and pesticides would be off limits.

Playing God under Glass

Gardening under glass is nothing new, but a 3-acre greenhouse in Arizona, with its own desert, ocean, rain forest, savanna, and farm, captured attention in 1991. Biosphere 2 was designed as a self-sustaining ecosystem, an enclosed miniature world in which plants, atmospheric gases, and animals—including eight *Homo sapiens*—would survive for two years in a balance simulating that of Earth (or Biosphere 1). The initial experiment was a resounding flop. To scientists, results were questionable. To gardeners, they were a nightmare. Microbes in the rich soil, imported from the Everglades, sucked up the atmospheric oxygen. Vines such as morning glory, which were to keep carbon dioxide levels down, grew out of control in the heady atmosphere and strangled food crops. All the pollinating insects died off, leaving the "crazy ants" to multiply like crazy. In 1996 a team of scientists from Columbia University took over Biosphere 2. Columbia's aims were modest: Students would spend a semester at the site studying various ecological issues. One scientist commented: "The best thing they'll learn is how hard it is to play God with this 3-acre parcel, let alone the whole Earth."

Young Frankenfood

There was nothing unusual looking about the big red tomato that hit supermarket shelves in May of 1994. But its appearance in selected stores marked a watershed in the history of vegetable production. Created by Calgene, a Californian biotech firm, the 'Flavr Savr' tomato was the first genetically altered whole food to be approved for sale by the U.S. Food and Drug Administration. To the retail industry, it was a dream come true. Here at last was a tomato that could be picked ripe and shipped ripe without rotting in transit. The secret? The gene that promotes ripening in natural tomatoes had been engineered to slow down. Opponents claimed that the 'Flavr Savr' might produce allergic reactions or unforeseen environmental damage and vowed to take the tomato to court. But a majority of consumers simply grew accustomed to the idea of genetic modification. "The key is that the flavor is there," said one Illinois supermarket owner, "and I don't see many consumers questioning how it got that way." The following spring, there was scarcely a murmur when a genetically modified crookneck squash—ominously named ZW-20—slipped into the supermarkets.

1995

The Edible Schoolyard

Alice Waters's passion for locally grown, organic produce was already well known when she turned her attention to school meals. As founder of the restaurant Chez Panisse, a gourmet's destination in Berkeley, California, Waters had defied commercial conventions by championing fresh, regional fruits and vegetables from farmers' markets. But educating well-to-do gourmets was not enough for Waters's crusading spirit. "Kids have to be taught that fresh, nourishing food is their birthright," she wrote, "that wholesome, honest food should be an entitlement for everyone." In 1995 she formed an alliance with the principal of the Martin

Gardening to Survive

By the end of the twentieth century, most Europeans and North Americans regarded vegetable gardening as a recreation—a healthy way of supplementing the diet with fresh, nutritious food. In Russia, on the other hand, the garden plot had become a means of survival. With the collapse of the Soviet Union, the unproductive collective farms—now officially joint stock companies—became even less efficient. Inexperienced private farmers struggled to make a profit on their inferior land (land that corrupt bureaucrats had reluctantly granted them).

For most Russian families, the only solution was to extend their private gardens in the suburbs or at their vacation *dachas*. Between 1990 and 1994, home production increased its share of Russia's total agricultural output from 24 to 38 percent. In 1998, private gardeners grew more than 90 percent of Russia's potatoes and 75 percent of its fruits and vegetables. One 1995 survey indicated that low-income families spent more than 700 hours a year in their gardens. Vladimir Bashmashnikov, head of Russia's association of peasant farmers, stoically took stock of the agricultural situation. "Things are getting better," he remarked, "but slowly."

Luther King Jr. Middle School in Berkeley and began transforming the school's run-down, 1-acre playground into an organic garden and outdoor classroom. Before long, student gardeners were tending a surprising range of vegetables, including mizuna, rocket, mache, fava beans, and heirloom tomatoes. Student cooks turned their produce into frittatas and calzones in the cafeteria kitchen. The Edible Schoolyard, as the project came to be known, aspired to provide the 900 students with a daily meal, ultimately creating "a school within a garden, rather than merely a garden within a school."

Seeds of Death

To the manufacturer, it seemed a stroke of genius, but for the poor farmer it was a nightmare—a seed genetically engineered to produce infertile offspring. Monsanto Corporation's new technology was still some years away from creating an actual seed, but environmental activists and farmers from less-developed countries were already raising an unprecedented storm of protest. "Terminator seeds," as they became known, threatened to reduce the farmer to virtual serfdom, while further concentrating the control of life in the hands of a few multinational giants. Surprised by the public outcry, Monsanto blinked first. "Because we thought it was our job to persuade, too often we have forgotten to listen," admitted Monsanto Chairman and CEO Robert Shapiro.

Easing the Greenhouse Effect

Years of comparing organic farming with agribusiness techniques yielded encouraging results as the millennium drew to a close. At the Rodale Institute in Maxatawny, Pennsylvania, where the field trials took place, researchers had long known that organic harvests of soybeans and corn were as plentiful (and significantly larger during periods of drought) as those grown with chemicals. What became apparent in 1999, however, was that the organic fields were soaking up greenhouse gases, as well. By converting soy and corn production to organic methods, it was estimated that the United States could reduce carbon dioxide emissions by up to 2 percent, an amount roughly equivalent to the total annual emissions of Denmark or Iraq.

1999

the
past
meets
the
future

Poison Pollen

While vegetables modified by fish genes (and other fantastic mutations) aroused visions of giant killer tomatoes, "BT corn" received less publicity. After all, the microbe *Bacillus thuringiensis* (BT) was a favorite organic method of controlling garden pests. What damage could it do when spliced to a plant's genes? The result was harmless to ladybugs and honeybees but deadly to a number of destructive creatures, including the corn borer. Within four years of its introduction, BT corn accounted for one-quarter of America's corn crop. Unfortunately, no one had consulted with the monarch butterfly. In 1999, studies by scientists at Cornell University revealed that about 50 percent of monarch caterpillars feeding on milkweed dusted with pollen from BT corn died within four days. Agriculturists were quick to underplay the dangers, but a threat to North America's most beloved butterfly was not easily dismissed. The millennium ended on a sobering note for the brave new world of plant science.

2000

Gardening Is Good for You

Finally it was official: Gardening is good for you! A study released in 2000 by researchers at Stanford University and the Universities of Minnesota and South Carolina found that exercise in the garden compared favorably to recreation that is generally considered more vigorous. Weeding and planting seedlings, for instance, require 4.5 METs. (One MET, or metabolic equivalent, equals the amount of energy a person uses while at rest.) This is the same activity level maintained while shooting baskets or walking at 4 miles per hour. Digging in the garden ups the MET level to 5.5, equivalent to playing doubles in tennis.

The U.S. Centers for Disease Control included gardening on a list of exercises that it recommended people do for at least 30 minutes a day. Gardeners were not surprised by the news that gardening was hard, healthy work, but after more than 11,000 years of digging, sowing, weeding, and harvesting, it was comforting to learn that they'd been doing the right thing all along.

Bibliography

Adams, William Howard. *Nature Perfected: Gardens through History.* New York: Abbeville, 1991.

Amherst, Alicia. *A History of Gardening in England.* London: Bernard Quaritch, 1896.

Andrews, Edward, and Faith Andrews. *Work and Worship: The Economic Order of the Shakers.* Greenwich, Conn.: New York Graphic Society, 1974.

Baker, Herbert G. *Plants and Civilization.* Belmont, Calif.: Wadsworth, 1970.

Balmori, Diana, Diane Kostial McGuire, and Eleanor M. McPeck. *Beatrix Farrand's American Landscapes.* Sagaponack, N.Y.: Sagapress, 1985.

Benes, Peter, ed. *Plants and People.* Boston: Boston University, 1996.

Betts, Edwin Morris. *Thomas Jefferson's Garden Book.* Philadelphia: American Philosophical Society, 1944.

Bray, Warwick, ed. *The Meeting of Two Worlds: Europe and the Americas, 1492–1650.* Oxford: Oxford University Press, 1993.

Brown, Jane. *Beatrix: The Gardening Life of Beatrix Jones Farrand.* New York: Viking, 1995.

Browne, Charles A. *A Source Book of Agricultural Chemistry.* Waltham, Mass.: Chronica Botanica, 1944.

Bruford, Walter Horace. *Germany in the Eighteenth Century.* Cambridge: Cambridge University Press, 1935.

Buchan, Ursula. *An Anthology of Garden Writing.* London: Croom Helm, 1986.

Buist, Robert. *The Family Kitchen Gardener.* New York: J. C. Riker, 1847.

Carolson, Laurie Winn. *A Fever in Salem.* Chicago: Ivan R. Dee, 1999.

Carson, Rachel. *Silent Spring.* Boston: Houghton Mifflin, 1962.

Carter, Vernon Gill, and Tom Dale. *Topsoil and Civilization.* Norman: University of Oklahoma Press, 1974.

Clark, Emma. *Underneath Which Rivers Flow.* London: The Prince of Wales's Institute of Architecture, 1996.

Clausen, Curtis P. *The Parasites of Popillia Japonica.* Washington, D.C.: Government Printing Office, 1927.

Cobbett, William. *The American Gardener.* New York: John Doyle, 1841.

Coe, Sophie D. *America's First Cuisines.* Austin: University of Texas Press, 1994.

Cohen, Joel E., and David Tilman. "Biosphere 2 and Biodiversity: The Lesson So Far." *Science,* 15 November 1996, 1150–51.

Columella, Lucius Junius. *On Agriculture.* Trans. Harrison Boyd Ash. Cambridge: Harvard University Press, 1977.

Commoner, Barry. *Making Peace with the Planet.* New York: Pantheon, 1990.

Cowan, C. Wesley, and Patty Jo Watson, eds. *The Origins of Agriculture: An International Perspective.* Washington, D.C.: Smithsonian, 1992.

Cruickshank, Helen Gere. *John and William Bartram's America.* New York: Devin-Adair, 1957.

Cuthbertson, Yvonne. *Women Gardeners: A History.* Denver: Arden Press, 1998.

"The Dawning of Earth Day." *Time,* 27 April 1970, 46.

Demos, John Putnam. *Entertaining Satan: Witchcraft and the Culture of Early New England.* New York: Oxford Press, 1982.

Devault, George. "Russia's Winter of Discontent." *Farm Journal*, December 1998, 18.

Dickie, James. "The Islamic Garden in Spain." In *The Islamic Garden*. Dumbarton Oaks: 1976.

Doughty, Roy. "The Edible Schoolyard." *The Ecologist*, May/June 1999, 210.

Dutton, Ralph. *The English Garden*. London: Batsford, 1950.

Ehrenreich, Barbara and Deirdre English. *Witches, Midwives, and Nurses: A History of Women Healers*. Old Westbury, N.Y.: The Feminist Press, 1973.

Erickson, Carolly. *Josephine*. New York: St. Martin's Press, 1998.

Evelyn, John. *Acetaria: A Discourse of Sallets*. London: Prospect Books, 1982.

Fagan, Brian M. *People of the Earth*. New York: HarperCollins, 1992.

Fairbrother, Nan. *Men and Gardens*. New York: Alfred A. Knopf, 1956.

Fairchild, Thomas. *The City Gardener*. London: T. Woodward, 1722.

Farrar, Linda. *Ancient Roman Gardens*. Stroud: Sutton, 1998.

Fein, Albert. *Frederick Law Olmsted and the American Environmental Tradition*. New York: George Braziller, 1972.

Fippin, Elmer O. "How to Get Along without Stable Manure." *The Garden Magazine*, February 1923, 220–22.

Flanagan, Sabina. *Hildegard of Bingen, 1098–1179*. London: Routledge, 1989.

Fletcher, W. W. *The Pest War*. New York: John Wiley, 1974.

Flint, Mary Louise, and Robert van den Bosch. *Introduction to Integrated Pest Management*. NewYork: Plenum Press, 1981.

Foster, Nelson, and Linda S. Cordell, eds. *Chilies to Chocolate*. Tucson: University of Arizona Press, 1992.

Fox, Matthew. *Illuminations of Hildegard of Bingen*. Sante Fe: Bear and Company, 1985.

Fox, Tom. *Struggle for Space: The Greening of New York*. New York: Neighborhood Open Space Coalition, 1985.

"Gardeners Who Armed with Food." *House and Garden*, November 1943, 60–62.

"Gardening: An Exercise That Bears Fruit in More Ways Than One." *Tufts University Health and Nutrition Newsletter*, June 2000, 3.

Golden, Frederic. "Of Corn and Butterflies." *Time*, 31 May 1999, 80–81.

Goldin, Owen and Patricia Kilroe, eds. *Human Life and the Natural World*. Petersborough, Ontario: Broadview Press, 1997.

Goody, Jack. *The Culture of Flowers*. Cambridge: Cambridge University Press, 1993.

Gothein, Marie Luise. *A History of Garden Art*. London: J. M. Dent, 1928.

Graham, Dorothy. *Chinese Gardens*. London: Harrap, 1938.

Grimshaw, John. *The Gardener's Atlas*. Willowdale, Ontario: Firefly, 1998.

Harlan, Jack R. *The Living Fields: Our Agricultural Heritage*. Cambridge: Cambridge University Press, 1995.

Haughton, Claire Shaver. *Green Immigrants*. New York: Harcourt Brace Jovanovich, 1978.

Hedrick, U. P. *A History of Horticulture in America*. New York: Oxford University Press, 1950.

Heins, Kathleen M. "Shaping Up to Garden." *Better Homes and Gardens*, May 2000, 284.

Henessy, Terry. "Buying Them by the Flat." *Progressive Grocer*, August 1994, 143.

Hightower, James Robert. *The Poetry of T'ao Ch'ien*. Oxford: Clarendon, 1970.

Hinde, Thomas. *Capability Brown*. London: Hutchinson, 1986.

Hobhouse, Penelope. *Plants in Garden History*. London: Pavilion, 1992.

Hollingsworth, Buckner. *Flower Chronicles*. New Brunswick: Rutgers University Press, 1958.

The Holy Bible. King James Version.

Homer. *The Odyssey*. Trans. Robert Fitzgerald. New York: Doubleday, 1963.

Hoyles, Martin. *Gardeners Delight*. London: Pluto Press, 1994.

———*The Story of Gardening*. London: Journeyman Press, 1991.

Howard, Sir Albert. *An Agricultural Testament*. London: Oxford University Press, 1940.

Howard, Robert West. *The Vanishing Land*. New York: Villard, 1985.

HRH The Prince of Wales and Charles Clover. *Highgrove: Portrait of an Estate*. London: Chapman, 1993.

Incas: Lords of Gold and Glory. Alexandria: Time-Life Books, 1992.

Isely, Duane. *One Hundred and One Botanists*. Ames: Iowa State University Press, 1994.

The Islamic Garden. Washington, D.C.: Dumbarton Oaks, Trustees for Harvard University, 1976.

Israel, Fred L., ed. *1897 Sears, Roebuck Catalogue*. Philadelphia: Chelsea House, 1993.

"J. I. Rodale and the Rodale Family: Celebrating 50 Years as Advocates for Sustainable Agriculture." [March 17, 2000] Available at www.dep.state.pas.us/dep/PA_Env-Her/rodale_bio.htm

Ji Cheng. *The Craft of Gardening*. New Haven: Yale University Press, 1988.

Karlsen, Carol F. *The Devil in the Shape of a Woman*. New York: Norton, 1987.

Kellaway, Deborah. *The Virago Book of Women Gardeners*. London: Virago, 1995.

Keswick, Maggie. *The Chinese Garden: History, Art, and Architecture*. London: St. Martin's, 1986.

Kiernan, Vincent. "Organic Farming Could Trap Excess Carbon." *The Chronicle of Higher Education*, 27 November 1998, 17.

King, Ronald. *Royal Kew*. London: Constable, 1985.

Knickerbocker, Brad. "Earth Day Has Helped Turn America 'Green'." *The Christian Science Monitor*, 22 April 1998.

Kolodny, Annette. *The Land Before Her*. Chapel Hill: University of North Carolina Press, 1984.

Koon, Ray. "This 'Organic Gardening' Business." *Horticulture*, May 1950, 183.

Kraft, Ken. *Garden to Order*. New York: Doubleday, 1963.

Kuck, Loraine E. *The Art of Japanese Gardens*. New York: Japan Society, 1941.

Leighton, Ann. *American Gardens in the Eighteenth Century*. Amherst: University of Massachusetts Press, 1986.

Leonard, Jonathan Norton. *The First Farmers*. New York: Time-Life Books, 1973.

Li, H. L. *The Garden Flowers of China*. New York: Ronald Press, 1959.

Liddle, Alan. "Alice Waters." *Nation's Restaurant News*, February 1996, 164.

Lind, Louise. *William Blackstone: Sage of the Wilderness*. Bowie, Md.: Heritage Books, 1993.

Lodeman, E. G. *The Spraying of Plants*. London: Macmillan, 1897.

Lodewijk, Tom. *The Book of Tulips*. New York: Vendome Press, 1979.

Loewer, Peter. *Seeds*. New York: Macmillan, 1995.

Lord, Russell. *The Care of the Earth*. New York: New American Library, 1963.

Lost Crop of the Incas. Washington, D.C.: National Academy Press, 1989.

Loudon, John C. *An Encyclopedia of Gardening*. New York: Garland, 1982.

MacFadyen, J. Tevere. "The Call to Dig." *Horticulture*, March 1985, 38–47.

MacKay, Alastair I. *Farming and Gardening in the Bible*. New York: Pyramid Books, 1970.

Maine Organic Farmers and Gardeners Association. [April 15, 2000] Available at www.mofga.org/mofga.html

Mandela, Nelson. *Long Walk to Freedom*. Boston: Little Brown, 1994.

McLean, Teresa. *Medieval English Gardens*. New York: Viking, 1980.

Milius, Susan. "New Studies Clarify Monarch Worries." *Science News*, 18–25 December 1999, 25–26.

Miller, Philip. *The Gardener's Dictionary*. London, 1735.

Molenke, Harold N., and Alma L. Moldenke. *Plants of the Bible*. Waltham, Mass.: Chronica Botanica, 1952.

Mollison, Bill. *Permaculture: A Practical Guide for a Sustainable Future*. Washington, D.C.: Island Press, 1990. [July 4, 2000] Available at www.permaculture.org.au

———. "The Terrible Time of Day." [July 4, 2000] Available at csf.colorado.edu/perma/yankee_intro.html

Montet, Pierre. *Everyday Life in Egypt*. New York: St. Martin's, 1958.

Moore, Samuel K. "Terminating the Terminators." *Chemical Week*, 13 October 1999, 9.

Moynihan, Elizabeth B. *Paradise as a Garden*. New York: George Braziller, 1979.

Netzley, Patricia D. *Environmental Literature*. Santa Barbara: ABC CLIO, 1999.

Noble, David Grant, ed. *The Hohokam: Ancient People of the Desert*. Santa Fe: School of American Research Press, 1991.

"Organic Fertilizer Can Cut Greenhouse Gases." *USA Today*, June 1999, 15.

"Organic Foods Production Act." *FoodReview*, September 1995: 9.

Osborne, Fairfield. *Our Plundered Planet*. Boston: Little, Brown, 1948.

Pemberton. J. H. *Roses: Their History, Development, and Culture*. London: Longman's Green, 1920.

Pincas, Stephane. *Versailles*. London: Thames and Hudson, 1996.

Price, Douglas T., and Anne Birgitte Gebauer, eds. *Last Hunters—First Farmers*. Santa Fe: School of American Research Press, 1995.

Price, Robert. *Johnny Appleseed: Man and Myth*. Gloucester, Mass.: Peter Smith, 1967.

Quintinye, Jean de La. *The Compleat Gard'ner*. New York: Garland, 1982.

Raeburn, Paul. *The Last Harvest*. New York: Simon and Schuster, 1995.

Rauber, Paul. "The Edible Schoolyard." *Sierra*, November/December 1997, 24.

Rice, Stanley. "Paul Berg." [April 16, 2000] Available at www.accessexcellence.com/AB/BC/Paul_Berg.html

Rodgers, Andrew Denny. *Liberty Hyde Bailey*. Princeton: Princeton University Press, 1949.

Rohde, Eleanour Sinclair. *The Old English Gardening Books*. London: Martin Hopkinson, 1924.

Roses for an Empress: Josephine Bonaparte and Pierre-Joseph Redouté. Trans. Anna Bennett. London: Sidgwick & Jackson, 1983.

Rossiter, Margaret W. *The Emergence of Agricultural Science*. New Haven: Yale University Press, 1975.

Salaman, Redcliffe. *The History and Social Influence of the Potato*. Cambridge: Cambridge University Press, 1985.

Sattler, Friedrich, and Eckhard V. Wistinghauser. *Bio-Dynamic Farming Practice*. Stourbridge, England: BDAA, 1992.

Scott, Christina M. "Seed Savers Exchange." *The American Gardener*, January 1999, 16–17.

Seeth, Harm tho, et al. "Russian Poverty: Muddling through Economic Transition with Garden Plots." *World Development*, September 1998, 1611.

Simmonds, N. W., ed. *Evolution of Crop Plants*. London: Longman, 1976.

Smith, Andrew F. *The Tomato in America*. Columbia: University of South Carolina Press, 1994.

Squibb, Robert. *The Gardener's Calendar*. Athens, Ga.: University of Georgia Press, 1980.

Stix, Gary. "A Recombinant Feast." *Scientific American*, March 1995: 21.

Tachibana no Toshitsuna. *Sakuteiki: The Book of Garden*. Tokyo, 1985.

"Tagari Farm." [July 4, 2000] Available at www.permaculture.org.au

Tanzer, Helen H. *The Villas of Pliny the Younger*. New York: Columbia University Press, 1924.

Thacker, Christopher. *The History of Gardens*. Berkeley: University of California Press, 1979.

Theophrastus. *Enquiry into Plants*. Trans. Sir Arthur Hort. London: Heinemann, 1916.

Thompson, D. B. *Garden Lore of Ancient Athens*. Princeton: American School of Classical Studies at Athens, 1963.

Tucker, David M. *Kitchen Gardening in America: A History*. Ames: Iowa State University Press, 1993

Tusser, Thomas. *Five Hundred Points of Good Husbandry*. Oxford: Oxford University Press, 1984.

"Twenty-Five Years after DDT Ban, Bald Eagles, Osprey Numbers Soar." [June 13, 1997] Available at www.edf.org/pubs/NewsReleases/1997/Jun/e_ddt.html

"U.S. Imposes Standards for Organic-Food Labeling." *New York Times*, 21 December 2000.

Vergano, Dan. "Brave New World of Biosphere 2?" *Science News*, 16 November 1996, 312–13.

"A Virginian Farmer." *Roman Farm Management: The Treatises of Cato and Varro*. New York: Macmillan, 1913.

Waley, Arthur. *The Book of Songs*. New York: Grove Press, 1960.

Waters, Alice. "The Ethics of Eating." *Whole Earth*, Summer 1997, 64.

Whorton, James C. *Before Silent Spring*. Princeton: Princeton University Press, 1974.

———*Crusaders for Fitness*. Princeton: Princeton University Press, 1982.

Yepson, Roger B. *The Encyclopedia of Natural Insect and Disease Control*. Emmaus, Pa.: Rodale, 1984.

Young, Alexander. *Chronicles of the Pilgrim Fathers*. Boston: Little and Brown, 1844.

Acknowledgments

Thanks to Scott Meyer, who wrote the article "A Brief History of Gardening" (*Organic Gardening* magazine, November/December 1999), which helped inspire the writing of this book. Thanks also to Maria Rodale, who enthusiastically supported this project; to Erana Bumbardatore, for her adept edits; and to Linda Brunner, for her patient attention to detail. Finally, many thanks to my editor and friend, Jennifer Hornsby, who took this book from seed time to harvest.

Photo Credits

A.K.G., Berlin/SuperStock, Inc. 6 (*Chapter 2*), 35 (A.D. 350), 50, 107

Algeria/Holton Collection/SuperStock, Inc. 6 (*Chapter 1*), 13 (10,000 B.C.), 17

James L. Amos/National Geographic Society Image Collection 213 (1990), 229

Heather Angel 159 (1865 and 1867), 175 (*top*), 176, 188 (1945), 203

Animals, Animals/Fabio Colombini 12 (24 million)

Archive Photo 206, 209

Archive Photo/Hulton Getty 7 (*Chapter 8*), 13 (6500 B.C.), 19, 58 (1050), 73, 82 (1452), 93, 186 (1918), 187 (1930), 193, 197

Archive Research International 161 (1909), 182

David L. Arnold/National Geographic Society Image Collection 58 (1080), 72

Bibliotheque Nationale, Paris/Bridgeman Art Library, London/SuperStock, Inc. 32 (500 B.C.), 39

Bridgeman Art Library

6 (*Chapter 4*), 82 (1375), and 88 (Ken Welsh/Palace of the Alhambra, Granada, Spain); 7 (*Chapter 6*), 134 (1753), and 140 (John Lucas Tupper/Oxford University Museum of Natural History); 32 (401 B.C.) and 38 (Bibliotheque Nationale, Paris); 34 (A.D. 64) and 46 (Pieter Gerritsz van Roestraten/private collection/Johnny Van Haeften Ltd., London); 34 (A.D. 100) and 49 (Giacomo Vignola/Villa Lante della Rovere, Bagnaia/Merilyn Thoroid); 35 (A.D. 138) and 48 (Visual Arts Library, London); 35 (A.D. 476) and 52–53 (Trevor Neal/private collection); 45 (from the 'Hortus Eystettensis' by Basil Besler/ private collection/The Stapleton Collection); 56 (630) and 61 (British Library, London); 57 (970) and 68–69 (Thomas Girtin/Ashmolean Museum, Oxford); 57 (1000), 70, 161, and 181 (designed by Sir Edwin Lutyens & Miss Gertrude Jekyll/Hestercombe House, Somerset); 59 (1250) and 78 (Pierre Croissens of Boulogne/ Livre des Prouffits Champetres et Ruraulx/British Library, London); 80 (Raffaellino da Reggio/ Villa Lante della Rovere, Bagnaia); 82–83 (1450) and 91 (Arthur Melville/collection of Andrew McIntoch Patrick); 85 (1556) and 101 (an English botanical manuscript/Bonhams, London); 86 (1597) and 104 (Herbert Johnson Harvey/private collection/Phillips, The International Fine Art Auctioneer); 108 (1617) and 112 (D. A. Greatorex/Chris Beetles Ltd., London); 108 (1631) and 116–117 (Yu Zhiding/private collection/Christie's Images); 110 (1693) and 124 (Pierre-Denis Martin/Chateau de Versailles); 111 (1722) and 127 (English School/Victoria & Albert Museum, London); 111 (1733) and 130 (private collection); 134 (1759) and 141 (Richard Wilson/private collection); 135 (1783) and 145 (John Bethell); 136 (1803) and 148 (Gilbert Stuart/private collection/Roger-Viollet); 136 (1817) and 150 (Pierre Joseph Redoute/Lindley Library, RHS, London); 158 (1847) and 166–167 (William Henry Davis/private collection); 159 (1854) and 173 (Sir Joseph Paxton/Guildhall Library, Corporation of London)

Rob Cardillo 12 (430 million), 13 (4000 B.C.), 14, 56 (840), 67, 83 (1493), 84 (1539), 85 (1574 and 1603), 92, 96, 103, 105, 110 (1682 and 1699), 114, 123, 126, 186 (1916), 191

David Cavagnaro 84 (1530), 97

Christie's Images 55

Christie's Images/SuperStock, Inc. 47, 57 (800), 64

Corbis 7 (*Chapter 9*), 14 (2700 B.C.), 26, 32 (563 B.C. and 750 B.C.), 33 (387 B.C.), 35 (A.D. 400), 37, 39 (*top*), 40, 52, 58 (1100), 59 (1200), 74–75, 77, 84 (1517 and 1550), 95, 98–99, 111 (1727), 128, 148, 158 (1840 and 1846), 159 (1856), 162, 165, 174, 175 (*bottom*), 184, 186

243

Index

Note: Page references in **boldface** indicate illustrations.

253